T0195748

HERE
for a
REASON

GOD DON'T MAKE MISTAKES

ROBERT MCLEAN

Order this book online at www.trafford.com
or email orders@trafford.com

Most Trafford titles are also available at major online book retailers.

Print information available on the last page.

ISBN: 978-1-4907-2951-0 (sc)
ISBN: 978-1-4907-2953-4 (hc)
ISBN: 978-1-4907-2952-7 (e)

Library of Congress Control Number: 2014904080

Trafford rev. 03/05/2015

 www.trafford.com

North America & international
toll-free: 1 888 232 4444 (USA & Canada)
fax: 812 355 4082

CONTENTS

Acknowledgement ix

My Memoir Key xi

Chapter 1   You Have to Learn Your Place (Little Boy) 1

Chapter 2   The Cajuns (Boy) 29

Chapter 3   The Day, the Devils Came to Town 91

Chapter 4   "You Are the Man, Until the Man Comes." 103

Chapter 5   David, You Got Balls 137

Chapter 6   Tennis Will Never Be Duplicated in a
             Hundred Lifetimes.. 169

Satire

Openly Disgrace 188
The Magnificent One (Then) 189
I Am Only a DJ, But (Now).. 194
Politics, an Ugly Business (Later) 211
Laugh to Keep from Crying (Forever More).................................214
Red Beard and the Black Tie (Eternally Fear Mongering) 220
Bugs in the Walls, Flies in Kee-Wee-Kar-Wah (Eternal Bliss)!.... 229
Openly Disgrace in Your Face (Closing) 238

Dear God, grant me one wish, do not call me to preach because you are hard on those who are supposed to know better.

Some proceeds will go to the creation of the *Annie B. McLean Mccoy|Doris Prince|Laura Welborn foundation*: A Place To Rest Your Head.

Some names and places have been change.

Acknowledgement

Mrs. Doris Jean Hollingsworth Prince: The hospice side of the shelter will honor Doris. Doris was like Mother Teresa, and with no place to go to, Doris's home was always open. Doris would pick up the homeless, take home, give showers, and say, "Eat and drink what we have and rest your head on my couches." Doris is love, and I always said, "She is my favorite cousin." Grave honor to name the homeless shelter on her behalf.

Ms. Laura Welborn: The medical side of the shelter will honor Laura. I have never met Laura. Laura is a good Samaritan who came upon an incident and handled it superbly. My son Robert was beaten and robbed by an animal driving a green SUV. There were broken bones in his face, eyes and nose were bleeding. Thank God, Robert protected his mouth that held his braces. In shock and about to be run over, Laura took over. Laura gave assurance and first aid. I called to thank her, but her soon-to-be husband was protective, and his right. I am honored to name the homeless shelter on her behalf.

My Memoir Key

Stories will make you happy, glad, or sad; continue on.

Stories will make you mad. *Change only after researching facts!*

Words will make you hot under the collar, cold and don't wanna (slave term) to be bother, warm to the touch, and cool so very much.

Your past will never change; however, with God all bad days are good days.

My past, I wish could change

My past, I wish could

My past, I wish

My past I, Robert Lewis McLean

CHAPTER 1

You Have to Learn Your Place (Little Boy)

A vivid recollection of my grandpa I carry. Grandpa would be sitting on the back porch in the morning sun. No one told me to sit with him. Grandpa would amaze me by staring. I would get behind him to see what he saw. I sat dangling my feet off the porch. I would catch him looking at me and quickly resume staring. One morning, I was going to sit; people were bringing Grandpa back in the house. People were holding him up as he could barely walk. Grandpa looked at me with something looked like white triangles in both his eyes. Grandpa gave me a very big grin, and I knew he was acknowledging me sitting with him. I went to my spot many days waiting for Grandpa, and I remember Mama saying, "Look at Lewis. He is waiting on Grandpa." Grandpa Mr. Lacy Hollingsworth and my baby brother who was named after him Sergeant Major Lacy McLean, Retired. (Acknowledge here and not the section; because, first priority of an army careerist is have a strong support system. My sister Mrs. Wanda Faye Palmer McLean, thank you.)

I have fond memories of my granny, Ms. Annie B. McLean McCoy, whom everyone called Miz Annie, including white people. Why the respect? Granny owned uptown land, and plans were concocted to get it. Three black people owned the majority of land: Granny, Mr. Thom Brice, and Mr. Harvey McClain, whose wife was a teacher. She told us education is the key to success. We did not take her

1

seriously because the color of your skin dictated your way of life. We could be cooks, busboys, porters, or lay tracks for the railroad. Even dream jobs like a policeman had its limitations "as blacks could not arrest white people. and being a fireman was a farce." If a white person's house was on fire, a black fireman could not help.

Our mind-set made Mrs. McClain mad, frustrated, and disappointed. She would take the song books out of the closet, slam down on the desk without hesitation, we would scramble to get one. We would turn to the song she loved. We sang "My Wild Irish Rose The Sweetest Flower That Grows." Afterward Mrs. McClain was a different person; she would say, "Put the books away and let's get to work, children." In the year 2008, Robert McLean cried in remembrance of "My Wild Irish Rose." I never thought in my lifetime I would see firsthand an education can propel you to be somebody special. Even the president of the United States.

I spent a lot of time with Granny, who treated me very special. By saying the words "please" and "thank you," most of the time I got what I wanted. Our regular routine, go uptown on Saturdays. My elder brother, Henry Lee McLean, whom we called Beau-friend, linked up with us. Black people had to enter through the back of stores. But not Granny. He wanted to see how it felt going through the front door. When we entered Efrids department store, we saw a brown bench on the right. Granny told us to sit there. "Robert, the pants you want need to be bigger 'cause the way ya growing you'll look like Abe Lincoln." "Beau-friend, who is Abe Lincoln?" "Lewis, he is a man who pants are so high he can walk in a foot of water and his pants won't get wet." I liked asking my brother questions because he always had all the answers. "Beau-friend why did Granny tell me if I wanted water to get it from that spigot?" (No cup, had to use my hands.) "White people drank form (word not misspelled) that thang?"

"That thang white people drink from is call a Coke machine, and I know ya love Coke, so get ya some." I went over, looked around, but not up. Wooden beams overhead, a man with a little pointed nose, big black glasses, looked like Tweety bird, I tah a putty kat, walked the beams observing black people as they entered the store. Store policy, a black could only enter after one exited, reasoning all black people steal, and Tweet bird (the name I gave him) could follow you. I took a sip ran back. Well! *Water!* Let it run awhile; the water will become sugar water, and a mix of molasses will turn it brown, wah lah you have Coke. I did what he said and ran back. Well? *Water!* Granny, Tweet bird and a bunch of white people were coming. I noticed Granny did not look happy. She grabbed me and started smacking my behind. I was screaming like she was killing me, and the white people were laughing. Tweet bird was making a jerking motion dance while Granny was hitting me. Tweet bird was enjoying this. Granny screamed, "Robert, ya are gonna hava to lean yo place, now git outside!" Beau-friend slipped away like a thief in the night. Later, Beau-friend gave me an apple; his way of saying sorry, and he had the larger one. "Lewis, did ya tell Granny I told ya to drink the water? I said "no." He said "well then change." I was little not stupid, Beau-friend hit harder than Granny. I had to hurry and bite. Beau-friend would eat the small one and say, "Ya know Iama Indian giver, so give it back." This time he was sincere, and I love my big brother.

Next Saturday, we went back to Efrids department store to see if the larger pants were back. When we got to the store, I said, "Granny, don't make me go in there. I never want to go in there again."

"Why, Robert?"

"Granny, I got a whuppin for drinking water. I never wanna (want) to go in there again."

"Okay, Robert, stand right there and don't move." Granny came into the doorway and said, "Robert, he says come in he'll give ya some candy."

"Granny, don't make me go in there." Okay Robert." Tweet bird tap the window. I looked up and he had the pants. I looked away.

He came to the doorway with some candy and said, "Robert, please come inside and try on the pants. I'll give you the candy." Tweet bird came, squatted, and said, "Didn't you like the pants? Would you please come inside?"

I did not look him in the eyes, because I was scared of white people's eyes. I would say why would God put cats' eyes in people? Tweet bird put his hand on my left shoulder to guide me into the store. I shrugged his hand off me and said, "Nobody touch me but Granny!"

Granny came out with the pants. "Robert, ya know ya should-hab come in tribe dese pants on. Dey donna fit I can'er (can never) takem back."

"Granny, you are the only person I know I say Granny. I don't want these pants. You can march right back in there, and nobody will say one word to ya!"

Granny turned her head and laughed. She then fixed her face and with a stern look saying, "Robert, I don't know what Iama (eye-ma) gonna do with you."

Tweet bird was devastated. Every time Granny shopped in his store for me, his plans to get a larger portion of Granny's land was in danger. "Robert, let's cross the street."

The sweet shop was in front of us. I started smiling. Granny was full of surprises. She knew the three things I loved: Coke, candy, and ice cream. Really, it was four things; I loved my Granny best. The front entrance had a sign I could not read, but I knew what it meant (Negroes go to the back, except Granny, her entourage, me). In the store, two men wore the common folks uniform (hat, long-sleeved white shirts, khaki pants). The majority of white men wore this. The two men in the booth were grinning as if playing a game of who will blink first. This was strange conduct even to a child loved to play games. The man behind the counter was big with pig-like face. "Pig face" stood on a platform, which made him look like a giant pig. All the stores paid homage to Granny. "Hi ya doing, Miz Annie? Hi ya feelings these days?" They all kissed Granny's ass because a lot of the uptown land was hers. I never did hear Granny speak; it was always one-sided. The big pop on the sign was five cents. Granny took the knot out of handkerchief and slid a quarter to Pig face.

Beau-friend was my mentor, who taught me the so-called facts of life. "Lewis, I'm gonna teach ya to count money because if you don't know what's in your pockets, niggers will steal it."

Pig face gave the candy, with fifteen cents change. I whispered to Granny. "My grandbaby says this is not right!"

Pig face started shouting, "I sorry, Miz Annie. I made a mistake. I not try to cheat ya!"

I looked at the two men in the booth still looking at each other, not smiling. Pig face put a dime down, and I whispered to Granny. "My grandbaby says this still not right!"

Pig face looked at me and said, "Well, boy, ya fix it!" I did like Granny. I slid the nickel to Pig face. I did not know my place. You hand white people money, and they would put it down for you to pick up. (Today, if I buy something, the clerk—black, white, or indifferent—puts my change down, not hand it to me, I'll buy something else. When they reach for the money, I put it down for them to pick up. Asian stores clerks use both hands as a sign of respect.) Pig face shouted, "I so sorry, Miz Annie, I was not trying to cheat ya! Miz Annie, please forgive me! God knows I was not trying to cheat ya!"

Outside the store, Granny said, "Robert, dust ya feet off. We are never coming back to this cracker store again. That cracker have been cheating me all these years. Robert, remember something— when a cracker tell ya he'za not stealing from ya, believe me he'za is!"

One morning someone knocked. Granny stuck her head out the door. "Robert, get up. Get dressed. We hava go. It'sa important."

I put on my new clothes and walked with a swag. (My God, kids today think swag is new) Granny said, "Look at my grandbaby strutting like a peacock." (I did not know what a peacock was, but he had to be a sharp dresser.) "Robert, stop walking like that. You betterah walk right. Ya not gonna go with me walking like that."

We went to the "Wilrik Hotel," which was for white people only. The place had bad odors, a mixture of stinking feet and bad breath. The hotel did not have plumbing. Big porcelain pots acted as toilets, by which, black people empty. Downstairs was a fountain shop from where we entered. "Robert, stand by the door so you can catch a breeze." It was hot, and the floor was railroad mats. Tar came out of the wood. Sand was put down to keep it from sticking to your shoes. An old man in uniform and three heavyset ladies with printed dresses used church fans to keep air circulation. A boy my size was playing on the floor. The boy had on grey pinstripe railroad overalls, no shirt, with tar and sweat on him. I thought, "I hope that boy do not come near me. He is nasty." The old man kept calling the boy, and whisper in his ear. Johnnie would come close. Finally, the old man reached in his pockets and gave Johnnie some money. He walked up to me with a circular motion with his right hand and said, "Hi'ya, Kingfish!" (*Amos 'n Andy* television show, white people in blackface portraying black people, and the con man who always get the worse of the deal was called Kingfish.) The old man was laughing hard, stretched out like he was going under the table. The three ladies were laughing mostly at the old man's conduct. The laughter stopped, and the boy turned to walk, away mission accomplished.

Printed in the United States
By Bookmasters

I cleared my throat, "Ahem!" As he looked back, I gestured, making a circular motion with my right hand, and said, "Hi ya, Cracker! The three ladies were looking at Mr. Nunnery with the church fans moving fast. The ladies bewilder looks on their faces became a challenge," you started this you had better do something that clean cut kingfisher just call my nasty boy a cracker!" I was shocked. I did not get the same response. Mr. Nunnery started rolling up his right sleeve as he struggled to get up. He was old, stiff, and needed a walker. He came toward me walking like a robot. Granny was talking with this tall white man, who had on the uniform of a businessman (black suit, white shirt, no tie or hat). She saw what had happened and knew I told her no one could whup me except her and Mama. No way Mr. Nunnery could hit me. I was too fast for him. I started bracing myself to duck and push him down. I had never seen Granny move so fast. She swooshed me outside.

"Robert, I'm gonna tell ya something, and ya better not forget."

"Sticks and stones can break ya bones, but words can never hurt ya."

"Now where ya get that from?"

"From you, Granny."

"From me!"

"Granny, you 'member at the candy store you says, 'Robert, dust ya feet off, we are never coming back to this cracker store again. Robert, that cracker been stealing from me all these years. Robert, when a cracker tell ya he'zas (he is) not stealing from ya he-zas (he is) 'member, Granny?'"

She had turned away a long time back. I knew she was laughing. Finally, she fixed her face with a stern look. "Robert, I'm grown. You cannot say or do what I do. Let's go home." Almost home, Granny said, "Robert, I want ya to let the neighbors know we are home."

Granny did not tell me why, and I did not ask. I liked showing off and made a grand, loud scene. "Granny, I think everybody knows we are home." As I went to inventory my toys, Granny slipped on a blue gown. She sat on the end of her throne, a blue leather cushion chair.

"Robert, that's good. Now come here and listen. Right 'fore it get dark, I want ya to go out the back door, get under da house, and when ya hear a knock, look around, get in da ditch, and go home. Robert, ya listen to me. If anyone calls ya, do not go to them. I want ya to run as fast as ya can, and Robert, do not come back he'rah. I can'ner (can never) help ya. Find a way home.

"Okay, Granny."

Beau-friend said, "it was so quiet here but no more. Look what the cat drug in!"

"Mama, ya miss me?"

"Yeah, right, where is Granny?"

"Granny home an she had me get under the house, come home up through the ditch. Somethang musta happen. I'll go see her tomorrow."

I was supposed to be napping when my aunt, Carrie Lee, came. She is the real Big Mama of the families. She takes care of her business and yours. Her motto, "I am Carrie Lee Hollingsworth, I drink cod liver, I don't take a lick (hit) off no black nigger!" (Ms. Sophia in the movie, played by Ms. Oprah Winfrey, carries the attitude of my aunt Carrie Lee.) She wanted to know what was going on. Mama said, "White folks wanted to take Miz Annie grand boy and teach him a lesson. Those white men are scared of a little Negro boy. They wanted to take him out hang him for drinking white people water. White man told him to do something three times, and he refused. On main street with people looking a white man had his hand on

8

his shoulder, and he broke away, screamed no one touches him but his granny and mama. Lewis corrected a white man who tried to cheat Granny. He didn't know the sign for the five-cent candy were for white people. He can charge black niggers what he wanted. Old man Nunnery, the grand man of the Klan, says he disrespect him and decent white ladies for calling their offspring a cracker. Carrie Lee, thank God the white man at the Wilrik Hotel told Granny the plan of the Klan. Carrie Lee, I think it's more to this, and only they and God knows. Granny says it came to light. Sheriff Holder came early in the morning. Granny was waiting for them. She did not lock her door. *Knock.* Granny says, 'Who is it?' 'Sheriff Holder.' 'Wat ya want, Sheriff?' 'Need to check for moonshine (did not need search warrant).' 'Sittin on the pot. Cum back later.' 'Miz Annie, comin in. Havta do my job.' Granny says, 'Well, the door not lock. I know it's not right for a man come in when a lady is on the pot.' 'Where is ya grandson?' 'Sheriff, I thinka those good white folks came while I sleep and took my grandbaby. I wanna ya to do ya job and find him. I am coming to ya place tomorrow and see if ya found him.' Carrie Lee, when the sheriff left, Granny got up off the pot where her moonshine was, locked the door, made her eggnog, and went to bed happy."

Granny said, "It's raining, bet on it." She went to Sheriff Holder. "I know ya came to get my grandson and turn him over to those good white men to be kill. Sheriff, don't let blood be on ya hands for killn' one of God children. He's just a baby. So, ya need to wash them now." The compromise was made with Sheriff Holder.

I was playing on the floor with my baby brother; someone was shouting.

Beau-friend said, "Lewis, that's Granny calling you."

"Coming, Granny! I miss you, Granny. It's been about two years!"

"Boy, ya know it's not been no two years."

"It's seems like it, Granny."

"Robert, listen to me. Ya can'er (can never) go back uptown (compromise) anyway. Those people are too good, and I have a new place, the dairy bar, 'cause I know ya like ice cream."

"Granny, you know people says that white man spits in your cone then put ice cream on top."

"We gonna have to watch him like a hawk, Robert."

"Yeah, Granny, 'cause I don't wanna eat somebody spit. I am gonna watch him like a hawk 'cause I don't wanna dust my feet off at the dairy bar."

Granny turned her head. I knew she was laughing. She turned back and said, "Robert, I don't know wat Iama (eye-ma) gonna do with ya. I just donna know."

We went across the railroad tracks which separated people on basis of skin color (people look white: but have Negro features, such as lips, noses and hair with zinc, have a community on the white side. We call the people Sand hills) to celebrate our reunion and my life (thank you, God and Granny, Robert McLean lives to tell what, when, where, how our land and livelihood were stolen). Black people could not go inside the dairy bar. Black people would go into an alley with a side window to order. Not Granny; we waltzed in, and homage was paid to Granny. "Wat it be, Miz Annie? How ya doing dese daze?"

"Give my grandbaby de vanilla cream on a cone." We watch him like a hawk spying a field mouse. "Thank you, Granny." We sat down, and a tradition I carried as a child, I offered Granny first. She would only take one lick. She knew I was watching her like a hawk (laugh). I would eat fast because my custom, have two. "Granny, may I have another one please?" "Please" and "Thank you, Granny" are the keys; she never says no. The ice cream man knew my custom, so I would change to a cup, not on top, and it was hard to spit in it as we would watch him like a hawk. When Granny turned her back, the white man would make ugly faces. She would turn back, and he would be all smiles. I did not tell Granny because I did not want to dust my feet off. We watched him, and the ice cream were delicious, especially without the spit. Granny could not read or write, but the volumes of books by Thomas Paine on "Common Sense" were experienced and played out in her lifetime. One day I said, "Granny, ya want to change seats? You always sit there."

"Why? He-za making faces at ya?"

"How you know, Granny?"

"I can see that cracker in da window. Come look!"

Yep, Granny knew and waited for time to expose him. "Robert, ya wanna dust ya feet off?"

"No. Granny, sticks and stones can break my bones, but ugly faces don't hurt me." Granny burst out laughing, sitting down with her feet running. She was screaming and spread her hand over her face, looking through her fingers. The white people who never looked at you were all eyes. This was the first time Granny had lost her composure, and it made me feel great.

Houses are on my land then and now. Granny was tricked easily as she could not read or write. Granny showed me the land she owned and called old man Makepeace a land grabber. "Robert, this is my road. The stake goes on the other side. That cracker moved it, ya 'member, Robert. Never forget that cracker trying to steal ya land."

"Okay, Granny, I'll be like a elephant love peanuts and never forget." She turned her head, and I knew she was laughing.

Granny would dress nice when she had business uptown. "Robert, go to Mrs. Poole house and wait for me." This was a white lady, and I went to the front door like Granny.

"Niggah! Get away from my front door! I don't answer my front door for no niggah. Go round back!"

Two black ladies in uniform gray dress with long white aprons were standing there. The younger maid said, "Come on, baby, I'll walk ya to the back door. You're hungry? Want something to eat?"

"Yes, mam!" I taste the sandwich and almost vomit. "I can't eat this. What is it!"

"Pimento cheese, baby." I had government cheese and it didn't taste like this. "You want a Coke with ice?"

"No, mam, no ice. Your house do not have a smell."

The ladies laughed, and the older lady said, "Miz Annie house have a smell."

"Yes, mam. Granny put those little white balls everywhere, and her house smell good and clean."

"Miz Annie grandson has lots of manners. He better or she will knock his block off, right?"

"Yes, mam."

The younger maid saw Granny and ran out to meet her. "Robert, ya come here without me, come to the back, okay."

Ms. Poole came in, kissing Granny's ass. "Have a cup of tea, Miz Annie? How are you doing?" She was talking to Granny, but I think this was the first time she saw Robert McLean. Granny did not answer her (the beautiful house is on Granny's land).

"Let's go, Robert."

"Granny, I am gonna dust my feet off here. She was mean and called me names."

"Robert, I can't take ya anywhere."

"Granny, I can stay home by myself 'cause I am a big boy (fast forward—my grandson, Beau said, 'Papa, I can do it I'm a big boy.' I laughed. 'Papa, is that funny?' 'No, I recall saying the same thing to my granny, when I was your age')."

"Robert, donna answer that door for anyone, yea hera me."

"Yes, Granny!"

Short time later, there was a knock at the door. I got off the bed and laid on the floor. A louder knock. I knew it was Granny testing me. A much louder knock, then "Robert! Robert!"

I opened the door. "Granny, I knew it was you."

"Good job. Now don't open that door for no one, yea hear me?"

"Yes, Granny, and you better not forget my name. You will be left out in the cold." Granny laughed and walked away, shaking her head, and I knew she was saying, "Wat Iama(eye-ma) gonna do with that boy."

I wish a hundred times I could tell Granny, "I love you." The signs of the time warranted when I told my beautiful mother, Ms. Lucille H. McLean, "I luv ya, Mama."

She replied, "Don't tell you love me. Show me. Go wash the dishes." If you had food, clothing, and shelter, that's love. My love for Granny was to make her happy and laugh.

"Granny, I knows you are laughing when you turn your head. Granny, it's okay to laugh." She gave me a big grin and nodded her head yes.

It was more than drinking white people's water and things taken as being disruptive to white society. Some of the good white people had an inkling Miz Annie's grandson will become a problem in the future. Mr. Slop Moore was in the sheriff's office. Someone snitched he has a liquor still in Jonesboro behind his pig pen. He overheard the Klan and passed the conversation on. "Sheriff, that nigger boy will grow up. He's the only link to this thang of ours. Let's teach (hang) him a lesson for the sake of our children. He just a little nigger boy. He'll forget in time."

"Nobody touches him. I given Miz Annie my word, y'all hear me!"

As a boy I would ask God many whys; as an adult, I still do.

"Granny, why you put on nice clothes? You don't have business uptown. It's not Sunday, no church day."

"Robert, can't I dress nice sometimes?"

The dress was off-white with purple flowers and very beautiful. "Granny, you got that pretty dress on. Are you gonna strut like a peacock?"

She burst out laughing. "Robert, ya don't stop, I am gonna whup ya."

"Granny, you only whup me one time, but it last awhile."

"You keep on, the next whuppin going to last ya a lifetime."

"Lifetime, Granny?"

"Yea, to ya get grown."

"Granny, why are you not taken your purse with the gray sack with the little mason jar you put the cold medicine that is put in the eggnog?"

"Granny, we come to this house, get the cold medicine, then leave. Why are we staying?"

"Granny, why Foster the bootlegger (I will not call him mister) give you moonshine, when I was distracted by that nigger (look out of the window at the pretty birds, is that a robin, look at that dog, Robert)."

"Granny, why are we going downhill? We stay uphill across the tracks."

"Granny, why the city not cover expose pipes in the black neighborhood?"

"Granny why was I rushing you? You always says walk fast?"

"Robert, know where ya going go come back and lock ya doors."

My heart is heavy as I struggle to finish this narrative. I cried then, now, and later. I had a caring grandmother who thought the world of me.

Granny had her hand on my left shoulder. "Come on, Granny, let's hurry." I moved when she stepped on the exposed pipe and fell. Ladies were on the porch fixing hair.

Ms. Elwood Tyson screamed, "Lewis, you made her fall! You was taking her too fast!"

I ran home screaming to Mama, "I made Granny fall!" As I write people stop and watch a grown man cry.

Mama said, "Lewis you didn't make Granny fall. She was drunk."

"Mama, I don't know drunk."

"Well, when you and Granny drink eggnog, what do you do afterward?"

"We go to sleep." My beautiful mother could have been a Supreme Court judge.

"Robert, case closed."

I had to go in this dark room. The only light was a brown lamp on the desk with a fat white man, brown suit, white shirt with top button not fastened. "What happened?"

"I took Granny too fast, and she slipped on that brown pipe."

"Was Granny drinking?"

"No, sir, I did not see Granny drinking. I wanted to hurry up so I could play with those kids."

"Go in the next room. Miz Annie is asking for you."

"Granny, I'm so sorry I was taking you too fast."

Granny put a curse on me. "Robert, one day you will feel the pain I am in." I was in unexplainable pain all ready. How could I hurt the only person I loved? I cried days and nights, no matter how Mama tried to sugarcoat by saying Granny was drunk. We went outside the box. We've never done this before.

Granny said, "Robert, come closer." The tall white man from the soda shop at the Wilrik Hotel was peeping at the door. This was the man who told Granny the sheriff and the good white people planned to kill her grandson. Granny put her land deed in my pants and pulled my shirt over it, and her last words to me on earth, "Robert, run!" I bolted out the door. The peeping white man grabbed me by the top of my shirt, took (strong-arm robbery) the land deed, and pushed me down away from the door so he could live the lie Granny gave him the land deed. "I got it! I got it!" The white people cheered like at a football game.

The plan worked except a flaw—not killing Mrs. Annie B. McLean McCoy's grandson. I got up and ran outside to my mother. "Mama, why did that white man take (strong-arm robbery) the paper from me? Granny gave me the paper showed me the land and told me old man Makepeace was a land stealing cracker!"

"Lewis, hush, hush now! Lewis, we are poor people. Granny didn't pay taxes. She signed for things. She didn't use money. (I did not know or realize Granny only had business with white people and she had assets: the white lady's beautiful house was on Granny's land. It was hard to believe Granny was not compensated and did these things because she had a good heart or her love and trust for white people.) Lewis, these white people want to settle her debt. I don't know where Robert McLean at. If he was here, maybe things would be different."

"Mama, Granny gave me her land, and when I get big, I'm gonna get it back!"

"I know you will, Lewis. I know you will. Now hush up watch. Silence can be virtual, and 'member God don't like ugly.)

(The actress I would love to play my Granny, Ms. Cicely Tyson.)

Granny's mama said, "When we drink eggnog, make sure the lamp is out."

"Robert, tell yo mama 'tis Annie B. McLean McCoy house. She runs hers. I run mines now. Robert, kill the lights."

"Okay, Granny."

"Say yo prayers, go to sleep. We hava lot do morrow."

Granny taught me the prayer "Now I lay me down to sleep." It was taught to her when she was a child. These beautiful words taught children to read, write, and memorize. A passage created in the year 1800 by Mr. Mac Duffie, a world-known bigot, who slighted the very poor, poor. (The man of today would be the nominee for president who said, "You are poor, because you want to be." Robert McLean say, "Nigger, please!")

I prayed over and over God might let Granny come back. Mama said, "Lewis, God not gonna let Granny come back, but I promise you will be with her again."

"I'm not gonna wait. I want my Granny now. I will not talk to anyone except Granny." Days went by all I did was pray. Structural prayers she taught me, even the time to eat. "Thank you God for the world so sweet," and she was amazing. Tell me once, and I will play it back.

Beau-friend came into my room. "Lewis, you and Granny had secrets, huh?" I nodded yes. "You and me need a secret too." We were the only ones home. I would not go to aunt Dorothy's, so he had to stay with me. Lewis our secret will be, looking over his shoulders. "You can only talk to me, okay?" I nodded yes. He shouted, "Okay!"

"Yes!" Mama said, "I'm worry about Lewis. He ain't talk in weeks."

Well, nobody here. Lewis talks too me. (A comic genius, Mr. Tommy Davidson, says, "How do you get smart with your mother when she is the smart one?") Mama hashed a plan to get me to talk, and it worked. The door closed, we thought Mama left for work. I went to my brother's room.

"Beau-friend, I kill myself, will I be with Granny?"

"No, you will only get a seat on that train that leave at midnight pack with people, and goes straight to hell. Lewis, that is the only train where Negroes are told go up front. The train goes closer to hell. It gets hotter with fire everywhere. When you get there, the doors are open. You are so thirsty you will drink anything. The devil will give Negroes sumthang to drink. It's kerosene. Negroes don't care and drink a lot to stop been thirsty. The devil give white people pitch forks and tell them to strike the Negroes in the butt. With all that heat and the kerosene coming out, now ya got niggers running around with their asses on fire!"

I laughed until my stomach started to hurt. I made it back to my bed. Mama stepped in the doorway. We thought she had left for work. I am sure she was in her room laughing because she did not scold Beau-friend for cursing. "Lewis, you look like you are withering away. You have a burden (depression) on you and Aunt Sarah James coming to help you for now."

"Mama, I miss Granny so much I hurt all over. I wish those good white folks would have kill me. I would hava ben in haben (heaven) with my shoes waiting on Granny. Granny says, me, her, all God children gonna hava shoes, and we gonna walk all over that haben (heaven)."

"Lewis, it was not God plan. God do not make mistakes. *You are here for a reason.* Why you call those people good when they were gonna hurt you?"

"Mama, that's me and Granny's secret. Granny say good, she mean bad. Granny says that is one pretty baby, she is really saying that is one ugly baby. You do that to fused (confuse) the white folks. I wish, I could tell Granny I love her a thousand times. Mama I can tell you I love you." This time she did not say, "Show you love me, go wash the dishes."

"I love you too, Lewis, so don't do anything to make us sad."

"I won't, Mama. I don't want my butt on fire." She laughed aloud, and I knew she had heard Beau-friend's story.

(God is fighting my battle to give back what was taken from me.)

Granny was true to her words when she said, "Robert, the next time I whup ya it will last a lifetime."

Mrs. Annie B. McLean McCoy (Granny)

Mr. Lacy Hollingsworth (Grandpa)
Mr. Buck Kelly (background)

HONORABLE MENTION

"Granny, people think you are so mean. They speak to you, and you don't say a word back." "Robert, when they say, 'How ya doing, Miz Annie?' they are talking at me, not to me. Robert, ya sho respect to old people by callin ther hole name. If people wanna me to speak, they hava to say, 'How ya doing, Miz Annie B. McLean McCoy?' ya understand?"

"Yes, Granny. I don't have to call you that long name, and you answer me. You know why?"

"No, Robert, why?"

"'Cause I call you my Granny!" She laughed. I scared her when I ran and gave her a big hug. She did not expect this and braced herself. She thought I was going to knock her over, and I noticed she did not know what to do with her hands. Out of instinct, she hugged me back, shaking her head, and I knew what she was thinking. "I don't know what I'm gonna do with this boy." Only one time I heard Granny speak. We met two beautiful young ladies. One had chubby cheeks, lime green blouse, gray pants, and was called Mammy Gal. The other lady had on a blue plaid shirt, blue pants, and her name was Ms. Evon Tyson.

Ms. Mammy Gal said, "Howya doing, Miz Annie B. McLean McCoy?"

Granny said, "Howya doing, ladies?"

"We're fine!"

Granny looked down on me and laughed because I did not know what to do with my hands and I was blushing.

"Beau-friend, I was not sleep. I heard you tell Mama our secret."

"Lewis I had to. All you did was stay in bed. I told you about hell. You still want to go? Oh man, you still thinking about it, I can tell. Well, sit down. I'm gonna tell you the real deal." Beau-friend did not give me time to answer. No matter, he was going to tell me a story about hell anyway. "Lewis, white folks are the devil children. I'm gonna prove it. Name me one good white person. Don't look at that Jesus's picture. I am not gonna believe he walked around that desert with no hat and looked like that."

"I don't know any, Beau-friend."

"Okay, I can understand that. It's a certain number. You get that number. You had better not go to hell. Name one mean white person."

"Mr. Nunnery was going to hit me for calling that nasty boy a cracker."

"That's one. Name another one."

"Ms. Poole called me names 'cause I went to her front door without Granny."

"That's two. Name another one."

"Tweet bird, 'member the store I drank white people's water?"

"Yeah, he does look like I tat I tah a putty kat." We laughed.

"That's three. Name another one."

"Pig face at the candy store."

"Oh yeah, we call him hog head. That's four, Lewis. If you name one more, you had better not go to hell. You need some time or days to come up with a name? It's okay."

"I don't need time. I have another one."

"Who is it?"

"Ugly face at the Fairview Dairy Bar. He was making faces at me when Granny back was turn."

"Lewis, that sumbitch can look natural, and he is the ugliest white person I know (easy, Beau-friend did not know any). Lewis, there is five mean souls waiting for you in hell. The devil only give his children pitchforks. In your case while they are waiting for you, he tells his children put your pitchforks in the fire until the tip is fire orange. If mean souls are waiting for you, a list is provided. Negroes on the list are not given kerosene. They are given gasoline. When you get there, the devil give his children the same instruction: 'Strike the Negroes in the butt.' Only this time with the fire orange tips pitchforks and the gasoline you drank, your ass explore! Now niggers are running around in hell talking shit. You get it? Talking shit!" I burst out laughing.

"Lewis, I should paint that Jesus picture."

"Beau-friend you must be planning on leaving home. You paint that picture you are gonna be in big trouble."

"You are right, Lewis. I can see Cille (seal) coming in here now shouting, 'Oh Lord, somebody done desecrate Jesus!'"

"Beau-friend, I don't know what that big word mean."

"That mean I messed up the picture."

"Beau-friend, you paint that picture, I know where you going."

"Yeah, Lewis, you are right. Lucille McLean will send me straight to hell, and I don't want to be there with my ass on fire, exploring, and talking shit with the restuva niggers.

"Lewis, it is two ways that is guarantee you will go to hell. Killing yourself and jacking off (masturbation). Jacking off will make ya blind. When the blind Negroes get to hell, the devil will give them prunes. You know, prunes make ya use the bathroom. The prunes are soaked in gasoline, so with the heat and the prunes working ya, now ya got niggers, shit fire!"

We laughed like there was no tomorrow. "Beau-friend, I was playing on the floor with the many toys Granny had for me. Granny was putting up a picture. She hit her hand, and she said, 'shit fire!' I looked up. She was staring at me. 'Robert, you say it, I'm gonna whup ya. (On this day May 29, 2012 the words ended a telephone conversation. The words are everlasting and brought back memories over fifty years of my beloved Granny.) The good white folks took my toys when they burned Granny stuff. Beau-friend, those kids were acting like they have never seen toys. Even two girls were in my toy box. A fat white man, tan suit, white shirt was in charge (clothing identify a man with clout. Regular business men wore black suits with white shirts.). White people only wanted something they had to take it to the fat white man (maybe this is the man Granny saw when she has business uptown). He gave a kid my fire truck. He threw it back in the box. The fat white man gave him my gray-and-red truck, and he offered it to me. The boy had a man face and needed a shave. How can this unshaven boy give me my own toy? I went to Mama with my head held high. 'Mama, they can take my toys 'cause I don't want 'em. I rather have Granny than those old toys.' 'I know ya would, Lewis, I know you would. I'm gonna get you more toys.' Mama, if ya get me something, I hope it's a Mickey Mouse watch.' 'Wow, my boy is growing up.' The good white folks built a fire to erase any evidence of how they accomplished taking my Granny possessions. Things they did not want were thrown in the fire, and with all the people watching they would look at Robert McLean and smile. My beautiful mother notice this as I grip her hand tightly. 'Lewis, remain silent. Sometimes the best words are those never spoken. Just remember this, God don't like ugly and this top the cake.' The beautiful trunk contents were thrown in the

25

fire, pictures, church bulletins, Bible (safe), and money. 'Robert, ya wanna hide ya money put it in the Bible leave it out. A thief will never open it.' 'Okay, Granny.' I laughed to show the people mean conduct did not bother me. I knew something very important. Mrs. Annie B. McLean McCoy was getting her stuff in heaven as it went up in smoke."

"Lewis, I did not tell you the stories of hell to scare you. I just wanna get cross to ya life is living." Beau-friend is heavy, and he is my big brother.

"Beau-friend, you know I am just a kid. How can I 'member all this?"

"Okay, Lewis, I'll break it down for ya. Keep ya ass out of hell!"

Acknowledgment: "Robert, you can't be a fireman."

"Yes, sir, Mr. (Billie Ray) Williams (teacher)." It was drilled in my generation: never question adults (disrespectful). My greatest hobby is to listen to the radio, then, now, and later. Many years later, the answer came from my favorite *The Tom Joyner Morning Show, Little Known Black History Fact*. "If white people's property is on fire, you are not allowed to do your duties as a Negro fireman. Do not conserve this way of life." The people of the time had it wrong. I'm sure a black person or woman had to be overqualified in order measure up to average. On this sour note, my blessing was granted. Take our great country back in time only if you go back as a woman or a black. Thank you, Mr. Tom Joyner and family. God bless you.

Note: To the reader, remember the key to my memoir, and I thank you with a challenge. I stayed away from writing this occurred December 1957. My belief, or I perceive the reader's mind-set, this may or may not happen. I challenge you to hug your spouse, child (cell phone, other devices to contact) and just say out of the clear blue, "Everything will be all right!"

Lucille H. McLean (Mother)

Henry Lee McLean (Beau-Friend)

CHAPTER 2

The Cajuns (Boy)

People in our neighborhood had light brown or dark complexion with straight hair. We knew them as the people who talked funny. Mr. Zellie (Z-Lee), the older man, was shown respect by all. A'Leous (Ar-lee-shows) was an Adonis. God made a beautiful man. As a boy who had not lost his innocence, I could not understand why women were not in his life. For a beautiful man, women should be everywhere. He excluded women and added men. It is mind-bogging even today, two type of men came to his house. Standing men and sitting men who always crossed their legs. One of the sitting men confronted A'Leous (Ar-lee-shows) (high-pitched voice) saying, "Why you treat us different when the other men comes? When those men are here, we sit all day. You never offer us a drink or something to eat. You are always catering to them. Why the favoritism?"

A'Leous said, "Well, bitcha, these men come here not offen (as spoken). They are visitors. You bicthas are here every minute of the day. You are like family, so if you want something, get it yourself. I am gonna tell you bitchas a secret. When real men are around, you havta payda before they pumpda, right, De'berry?" The standing men burst out laughing, pointing to Mr. De'berry Southerland.

I should make another category a squat man. The standing men started ribbing Mr. De'berry Southerland. "Dee, ya got two notches on ya belt. We know of Little Richard, and now A'Leous." Mr. Ishmael Buf'fin, a black Algerian American Frenchman (my first super hero) said to Mr. De'berry Southerland, "E-fen-day(friend), monsieur la Ric-chard ista rich, howeze mucha monsieur payda for de-serviceda?"

ISH (E-she), "Little Richard is so pretty I fucked him for free."

Mr. Billie Marsh shouted, "A'Leous, bring Dee a jar of his own! You know the saying of the day. 'A man that will plug a butt hole will suck a pole,' and Dee got some mighty fine pussy lips. I'll bring a jar back, darling, 'cause this bitcha don't make a move soon, I'm gonna cut her too thin to fry or to thick to boil."

The outspoken sitting man uncrossed his leg, jumped up, hugged, and rendered an apology for his rudeness. Mr. De'berry Southerland said, "Prison ruin my life. I'll crawl over ten pussies to get to a dook-shoot (rectum)." The men laughingly told A'Leous to hurry with the jar and bring a chair for his newfound friend. New! *Mon' cheri* (my sweetheart) ista old hand. The men called Mr. De'berry Southerland a backslider. Once the moonshine kicked in, the men would show an acquired talent for singing. I called this singing group "standing men and a squat man." Mr. De'berry Southerland had a tenor voice and sounded like a sitting man, Mr. Johnny Mathis. Mr. De'berry Southerland could blow (pun intended) the roof off the sucker. The men were the first rappers. I recalled a poem recited by the standing men. They would talk after each other giving a spend on the narrative about down in the jungle deep a lion step on a monkey feet. The best poets were schooled in prison and would say, "Prison ruin my life."

Mama came to my hideout (little hallway closet) and gave me a warning. "Lewis, I don't like ya listening to the men."

"But, it stays at A'Leous."

"I don't wanna hear one word outside this house, ya hear me?"

"Okay, Mama." (I am true to my beautiful Mama. This is the first time ever spoken or written.)

A'Leous said, "Cille (seal) ze ista only female friend I hava, and I will treat ze liken my sister. We hava leave bot year how-ze liken stay in my house with no bills to pay? I hava nough food to last til I get back. Ven I get back ya hava move." Mama was happy to live a year without bills."

The house was made of railroad mats (wood, tracks were placed on). This was the best house ever. The neighbor (Heck family) across the road had a mountain tree which covered the houses. In Ssummer the house would get cold, and you had to go outside to warm up. In winter, you had to make a small fire; the house would get hot, and you had to go outside to cool down. We spent more time outside than inside a remarkable house.

The year went by fast. A'Leous came back first with a goat. "Cille, you know wat I said, 'Wen I return.'" A'Leous thanks this was a blessing.

"I got to save a little money, and feel I should give ya some."

"Ya can't do that, Cille. What are friends for? Y'all keep my house safe. I couldn't take it with me."

We had a place, the red house across the tracks. The weather conditions of the red house were opposite of A'Leous's house, but we still spent a lot of time outside. The Cajun men came back with a large trailer filled with animals' hides. It was the first time I saw beaver, mink, and bear. The light complexioned Cajun with different color eyes (blue and brown) had a skunk hat. He chased the children pulling up the tail, and we ran for dear life.

Sheriff Holder drove up with a little man who had a pointed head. I immediately gave him the name Peanut (today he would be Mr. Ross Perot). The men were speaking French and shouting. Peanut tricked the men, and A'Leous tried to throw blue paint on the furs. Peanut said, "Take what I offer, or the sheriff will take the furs and arrest you all for bringing the furs across state lines." A heavy man sat on A'Leous's chest. Peanut wore the uniform of businessman: black suit, white shirt, no tie or hat. Regular white men wore white shirts and khaki pants. In A'Leous's house I noticed some sitting men wore plaid shirts with khaki pants. I thought this was better because the colors blended or matched. Mr. Zellie (Z-lee) and Peanut closed the deal with advantage to Peanut. Peanut smiled, and Sheriff Holder drove away with the furs. Mr. Gerald Staten and Mr. William (Fang) Marsh dads were drinking moonshine and talking loud, not realizing people made money and points for reporting to the police.

"Mr. Zellie, the people going back hold them up. We are gonna get your stuff back," said Mr. Floyd Staten. "We know (e)xactly where they takum." They went to get the hides, but the grapevine news from the hood got to the sheriff and Peanut first. They took the furs to a safe place, a jail cell. No hides or furs—they thought it is a lost cause. Lord and behold! Another building not locked with the lock dangling on the hinge. Sheriff Holder and Peanut forgot to lock the building in haste. They went in and founded wall-to-wall prize blue ribbon hams. One small ham was left in the center of the building. They did what Sheriff Holder and Peanut forgot; they locked the door. The majority of hams were given to the returning Cajuns. They were happy. "Hams will bring a bigger price. Everybody have hides. Hams are rare. It's like a gold mine," said Mr. Zellie.

Mr. Floyd Staten and Mr. Billie Marsh did a remarkable feat; they refused to take the money offer. "We didn't get the hides, so we not taking money." The men shouted in French, pushing each other which was fighting back in the day. A'Leous said, "They feel bad you gave them the hams and not take ze money. They say you are beautiful people want to give you something in return and not leaving until something worked out."

Mr. Floyd Staten said, "Tell them these hams are hot (e)nough to cook by themselves. They need to get some miles away from here. Tell them you gonna make a meal in our honor since people say ya are a good cook. Now prove it."

A'Leous told the men. They shook hands, hugged, and said, "*Ob-wah*." The Cajun with the different color eyes was hugging Mr. Billie Marsh a long time. A'Leous said, "Y'all need to get a room." Everyone laughed except me. I did not know the meaning. Someone called from the tracks. "Miz Lucille, A'Leous says come help."

"Let's go, Lewis. You better behave."

"Okay, Mama."

Mama opened the door, a cloud of smoke and aroma rushed into the house. The hood were cooking ham. Somebody had left a bag at our front door. Mama said, "Christmas have come early this year." It was a foot-high sliced quarter-sized cure ham, which may be eaten without cooking. "We are not taking anything. Lewis, you think we should take this ham?"

"No, mam, we are helping, so we don't have to take nothing."

"Lewis, you try to be so smart."

"Thank you, Mama."

"Don't make me undress ya before we leave."

"Yes, mam."

33

A long table with white sheets that almost touched the ground held many dishes, and people were bringing more food, excluding ham. All of sudden, Sheriff Holder's big black sedan sped in the yard and stopped, making a cloud of dust. Peanut jumped out shouting, "Niggers! Nigger! I hate niggers! I smell ham ten miles away. I know you niggers stole my hams. You niggers going to pay! Old nigger, young nigger, men, women, and nigger bastard children, y'all going to pay!" Peanut kneeled in front of the car, panting like he could not catch his breath. Mama said she thought "that little white man was gonna have a heart attack."

Sheriff Holder called Mr. Billie Marsh. "Hey, Marsh boy, git over herah (here)." Mr. Billie Marsh did what was ordered. Chewing tobacco spitting in Mr. Billie Marsh's face, The sheriff said, "I know ya stole dem there hams. Ya didn't steal 'em. Ya know who done it (literacy never discriminate)." (Sheriff Holder's hood name was a cartoon character because of his fat belly and the location of the little gun "Deputy Dawg." Today Sheriff Holder would be The Honorable Governor of New Jersey.) The tobacco juice was coming down like rain. Mr. Billie Marsh stood at attention, not moving. Sheriff Holder looked at me as I picked up a rock.

"Lewis, you better not! You better behave!" Mama stopped me. I was going to throw and run. Granny had told me about a little boy my size who took a rock, slew a giant, and cut his head off. I thought, "I am David. I will hit the fat sheriff between the eyes with the rock. Someone else have to cut off his head. I'm just a little boy."

The sheriff had short arms also, and he struggled to pick Peanut up. "Peanut, stop crying." He gained his composure, and as they were leaving, he made a lasting statement. "You niggers, the next time you steal my hams you are going to die because I am going to poison them! All right!" That little white man did say, "The next time."

"Wat a idiot," said Mr. Floyd Staten. Mr. Billie Marsh was crying. A'Leous came with a pail of water and started cleaning him up. Seeing my mother cry, I cried with many others.

He shouted, "Why y'all crying! Don't cry for me! Don't cry 'cause that cracker spit on me. I was crying, I thought these was my last days on earth. I said to myself, 'please God I have a lot of stuff to do.' I was crying I thought I was going to die. That cracker breath smell like he's been eating dog shit! God help me!" Everyone burst out laughing. Someone gave Mr. Billie Marsh a small mason jar of moonshine, and he drank it all. He looked at the crowd and said, "I only have one thang to say, do we have any of that turkey left?"

The crowd shouted, "We got plenty turkey left under the table!" The sheets were lifted, and trays of ham were placed on the table. (Today, I go to the grocery stores and make a special trip to the meat section just to look at the "turkey ham.") Mr. Sam Sumthin, the greatest harmonica player ever, played a song fitting the occasion, "Turkey in The Straw," by which we danced, made henhouse noise, strutted, and sang well into the night. Of course, I found a way to get into trouble by shouting, "Any cock key doddle do." My mother made me sit down before I got a beat down for acting mannish. (Remember in hood talk, the primary word is opposite. In the military, I was approached by two white soldiers. "McLean, you are from the south, right? Tell Petersen you all call pussy cock, right?" "Naw, man, we call it as we see it." "I tell you why I will have to kill you. I am going to spare your life. A Negro would be kill if an old ugly white woman say you whistle at her. Killed for saying the wrong word or looking at white women, any menial thing. The keyword is opposite to confused white people." I say, "Johns, you are a pretty motherfucker." He turned red-faced, and Petersen burst out laughing. "You are not really saying that, right McLean?" "Right on!") The hood came together as one. I wondered how the informers felt when Sheriff Holder spit on a black man. We are judged by the color of our skin (thank you, Reverend Dr. King). (Mr. Dave Chappelle, a man of comedy had a block party in New York City and had many acts.) We had one act, Mr. Sam Sumthin. Back in the day, a singer or musician was above the rest. The people would say he or she sold their soul to the devil. Watching the movie where the beautiful Ms. Beyonce is depicted as the late (diva) Ms. Etta James, I thought the harmonica player Lil' Walter is a replica of Mr. Sam Sumthin.

A'Leous showcased his food preparation and cooking skills. He went to the standing men with a black handle pot. "This what I'm fixing for us. Thought you brave men would like to try this (talking like a lady). It is call craw fish."

Mr. Floyd Staten said, "I'll try anything once. How ya eat this?"

"Ze best part is ze juice. Bite ze head off and suck."

The men all shouted, "Oh hell! No!" The men laughingly tried to get Mr. Billie Marsh to do it. Mr. Billie Marsh said, "I'm drunk but not that damn drunk. I ain't biting or sucking on a damn thang."

A'Leous walked away, saying in a lady-like voice, "Donna knock this, it's good for ya specially that swinging Richard."

The men laughed, and Mr. Floyd Staten said, "That damn A'Leous always trying to get in our pants."

A'Leous pointed to some dishes and said, "These two (dishes) dis-sa hot with Cajun peppers, donna giva children."

"Mama, I'm gonna try the hot one."

"Go head, Lewis. You know a hard head makes a soft behind."

On stage, I got to be brave so I tasted. An Indian war dance hitting my mouth saying, "Wa, Wa, Wa!"

"What Lewis saying?"

"I say water, you fools! Water!" The party laughed timidly. I came to the conclusion it's too early, real people would come out after consuming moonshine. I mixed the dishes and created "Spicy." Grownups say it's very good.

Children shouted, "Lewis, fix mines."

"Okay, little people, get in line."

Mama whispered, "Lewis, don't give the babies the hot one, okay."

"Okay, Mama."

Sheriff Holder spitting tobacco saliva on Mr. Billie Marsh. Mr. Charles X Cotton Picker as called by the standing men was sitting, hitting his right hand on his right thigh. He was a standing man, and it was quite rare for him to go against the norm. The men stood in front of him, blocking the sheriff's view. Mr. Charles X Cotton Picker walked with a limp; one leg was longer.

I sneaked to Mr. John Robinson's pool room to get money from Beau-friend. Beau-friend got his name from the Frenchmen. "Beau" means beautiful in French. He cut wood and stacked it in a lock shed. "Lewis, ya better make sure it's locked. Don't trust no nigger."

Mama said, "Why ya still cut wood for them, and they have not paid ya?"

She did not know he got paid in advance, and wanted to have control of his money. Maybe she did and wanted to see what was in his heart. "Cille, it's my job!" Beau-friend and my brother Mr. Calvin Eugene, whom we called Genie Boy (today he is call Juice), call Mama Cille. It did not take me long to realize when you said, "Cille, may I have a nickel?" she did not hear you. "Mama, may I have a nickel?" got instant actions; you might get a dime. The Frenchmen christened my big brother "a beautiful (beau) friend."

Bro Ditty Smith racked the table, collected money after each game. He said, "Beau-friend would be back later. Lewis, sit on that bench. If the police come in, get up and leave. Don't sit there."

"Okay, bro Smith." Beau-friend ran errands for the men at work (gambling pool, cards, dice, numbers from the newspaper published for the day). The men started talking; somebody threw a brick and burst the big window at the police station.

Mr. John Robinson said, "All y'all got those old hawk bill knives putt 'em in this drawer. Ya know the heat will be on til they find out who did this." No one stepped forward. Men who had knives were labeled a coward in the hood. Win a fight, pull a knife in the eyes of the hood you lost and shame on you. The outside door to the poolroom closed by itself. It was very slow and made a screeching noise. Mr. Trick Knight ran into the poolroom, slid on brakes, turned back to the slow-moving door, and shouted, "Close that door and close it quick. Some sumbitch done threw a brick!" The men went crazy with laughter and rolled on the floor, smacking each other's backs. I laughed at the men's childish actions the first time I experienced this in my young life. I looked right and saw shining black shoes. It was the police, a black man and two white men. I got up, made eye contact with the burly white policeman close to me. The men stopped acting up.

Outside, I turned back to the slow-moving door (the devil made me do it; thank you Mr. Flip Wilson), and shouted, "Close that door and close it quick. Some sumbitch done threw a brick!" I heard an uproar of laughter. I ran to Wall Street Baptist Church. The police came out of the poolroom looking for me. I ran down Foster Alley to Aunt Dorothy's house, where I was supposed to be. Mrs. Agnes Hollingsworth Brooks would keep us. She is just as nice today as she was back then. All she had to say was "I'm gonna tell ya mama." Stop cutting up; she would forget. You wanted your mother to discipline you, not Aunt Carrie Lee. She showed no remorse. She still might whup your ass for general purpose (GP). Somebody told the police it was me and where I ran.

The black policeman told all the children, "Come out! If you don't, and I have to come get you, you are going to jail." The burly policeman was looking at me.

Old black Mac said, "You see him?"

"Naw, I don't see him."

Agnes said, "Lewis, that policeman was looking at you. Was it you?"

"Yeah, Agnes. Now Mama gonna tan my behind for messing with the police. I know somebody gonna tell."

"This is our secret. Nobody tell on Lewis. The only way she find out you tell."

"Hell, Agnes, I'm not gonna tell on myself."

"Lewis, ya keep cussing. I'm gonna tell."

"Okay, Agnes, I'll stop."

"You had better."

It was only fitting my beautiful good-hearted relative would marry a man of equal values, Mr. Tyrone Brooks, Ms. Gladys Brooks son.

Beau-friend said, "Lewis, people want to see ya at the poolroom, so come on." The men had a large wine bottle called "Roma Rocket." It dawned on me as I write my memoirs I never saw anyone take a drink. The men were looking at me, grinning as my brother guided me to the front. Mr. John Robinson and Mr. Charles X Cotton Picker were smiling. The first thing I noticed was Mr. Charles X

Cotton Picker's shoe; it was stack high. He hugged me, and the men went swoosh.

Mr. Trick Knight shouted, "Close that door and close it quick. Some sumbitch done threw a brick." The laughter was deafening. I looked over my right shoulder before I laughed, and the men started imitating me, looking over their shoulders and laughing. I got a cup to get some wine.

Beau-friend said, "Oh hell, no! Lucille McLean not gonna kill me ya get Nehi grape." When the police came after me, men with contraband got a chance to hide it. (This was a thank-you gesture for saving the day and also a way out for the police.) Mr. John Robinson gave me a red coin purse filled with money.

"Lewis, you know what I said about money in your pocket. It still stands. Get home, count it."

"Mr. John Robinson, I would like to buy a bag of peanuts."

"Put your money or our money away, Lewis. It is no good here." He gave me two bags. I looked at my big brother as I thanked Mr. John Robinson.

"Lewis, take ya ass home!"

"Okay, Beau-friend." The writing on the wall: Mr. Charles Cotton retaliated for the way Sheriff Holder treated his friend, Mr. Billie Marsh.

A'Leous was fixing a meal, and the standing men were outside, talking. "The way that little white man was acting, I wish we had taken the little ham left in the center of the building."

"Da daa, your wish issah granted!"

"What! I went back, got the ham, filled the bag, and hung it back up. That was the sweetest meat I ever tasted. I would love to see his face when he get a ladder and take it down. Surprise! Cow shit!" We burst out laughing.

After the meal, A'Leous said, "Y'all come in the kitchen to pick what food ya wanna take home. Y'all look." He moved a piece of cloth that covered a tub of candy underneath the sink. "When yo mama go to the home brew party, I'll babysit ya." Mama got up to see why we were detained. He hurried and dropped the cloth.

At home she asked me, "What did A'Leous say when ya was in the kitchen?"

My reputation is I do what Mama says and never lie to her. I told her what A'Leous said in its entirety. "Lewis, I got candy here, but you eat too much, not your food. That's why I hide it. Genie Boy, go get me a switch."

"Why, Mama!"

"You got a hard head, and you will go to that man house after I tell ya not to."

"Don't whupp me, Mama. I'm not gonna go!"

"Lewis, you stop him. If you can't, run and tell Carrie Lee he went to that man house."

"Okay, Mama." Genie Boy would have said, "Why, Cille?" His ass would have been whup like there was no tomorrow.

Mama watched as we went to Aunt Dorothy so Agnes would keep us. We had just started playing; Mama returned and took us home. She had the look, yes the look "don't say anything, Lewis, I'm not in the mood." There was a knock at the door; she motioned for me to answer.

"Who is it?"

A voice like a lady's said, "It's A'Leous. Open ze door, Lou'wis (Lewis)." Mama at the door had the largest knife I had ever seen. Only once in my lifetime I heard the voice Mama spoke. She sounded like the late great singer Mr. Issac Hayes, only deeper.

"A'Leous, you befriend me. You are after my boys. You get away from my house now!"

"Cille, it's not like that (voice changed back)."

"A'Leous, it is like that. You step foot one foot in my house, I will kill ya! I'll tell you again, get away from my house. All the time we know each other you never came here. What so special? Why tonight? Ya come in here, I will kill ya!"

He did not answer because his intentions were not good. He stomped off the porch and sat on the railroad tracks facing the house. "Lewis, you see him?"

"Yes, Mama."

"If he come this way, let me know."

"Okay, Mama."

He sat on the tracks pitching rocks, facing the house with a sad look on his face. The McLean family missing, Beau-friend were ready to fight. Mama had a big knife. I had a fork. Genie Boy had clenched fists. Beau-friend had left earlier dressed to the nines or people would say he was cleaner than the Board of Health. He, Mr. Harry Smith, Mr. Crybaby McLeod, and others had formed a club called

The Four F'ers. While leaving, he said, "Lewis, let Cille know I'll be at the clubhouse corner Wall Street and South Steele Street (Bland Drugstore) if y'all need me."

A'Leous sat on the tracks, contemplating what he was going to do to get those children by any means necessary. (Thank you, Mr. Malcolm X.) The neighborhood watch committee lived up to expectation. He got up and make a hand motion, forget them. Someone let the party know, there's a problem in the hood. He saw Aunt Carrie Lee and people leaving Miz Mary Durham's house party coming to the rescue and hightailed it (pun-intended). Aunt Carrie Lee shouted, "Cille, what the hell going on here!"

"Carrie Lee, sit down, and I'll tell ya."

"I don't know if I will. My feathers have been ruffled." People politely asked her to sit. You did not want to push your luck sounding hostile or combative. Aunt Carrie Lee would open a can of whup ass on anyone.

"I watched my boys as they went to Dorothy house. While at Miz Mary Durham party, a man I never saw before was talking about a hanging. He was talking to the people setting by the front door. It seems like he was talking to me personal. He said, 'They found that little white man hang in his smokehouse.' We all know hanging is a white man game. The Cajuns are nervous white people might think they did it and pulling up stakes. Everyone leaving except Mr. Zellie. He said, 'I'm old, tired, go back, I'm staying.' The little white man ripped off the Cajuns. The man he sold the hides ripped him off and told the white people he's a Jew. The man said, 'I believe the white folks kill him, 'cause they say a Jew is nothing but a white nigger.

"I started to take a sip of whiskey. It came rushing to me they are leaving, did not tell anyone. He wanted my boys to go to his house. Don't let seeing your boys going to Dorothy be your last memory.

You had better go get your boys! I put the glass down, went got my boys. A'Leous shows up to take my boys."

"Cille, I'll go beat that pretty man!"

"Carrie Lee, I handle it. Now sit down and don't get in any trouble. They came in peace. Let them leave in peace, and thank God he did not leave with my children."

The house was filled will people. When something happens in the hood, it spreads like wildfire. Aunt Carrie Lee said, "Cille, you was ready to fight. What was your boys doing? Cowering in that corner, crying?"

"Not my boys! Genie Boy had his fists ball up, and Lewis had a fork."

"A fork! Lewis, wat in the hell you gonna do with a fork!"

"I was gonna stick 'em in the face. I was gonna stick 'em in the stomach. I was gonna stick 'em in the leg. I was gonna stick 'em in the butt!"

"Lewis, you stick 'em in the butt. He might like that! He's a sissy!" The house went up with laughter. I had the green light to perform. Mama was laughing, crying. She said, "Thank you Jesus, it is not a void in my heart." The laughter slowed down.

"Lewis, where ya gonna stick 'em?"

I would say fast, "In the butt," same response.

Mama said, "Lewis stop, or I'll get a shoe thrown at me and y'all children go to Dorothy."

Aunt Carrie Lee was watching and knew I had to close the act. I mouthed the words, and she burst out laughing, and a shoe sailed by my head.

We said, "Mama need glasses. She never hit us."

I do recall that she said, "I'm gonna throw shoes at ya, not hit ya with them (mothers are the smart ones, thank you, Mr. Tommy Davidson, comic)."

Sitting on Aunt Dorothy's steps, the kids picked up. "Lewis, where ya gonna stick 'em?"

"Real fast in the butt." They laughed loudly, making noise and woke up the baby Doris Jean.

She came out the house rubbing her eyes, came to me, and with a loud baby whisper in my ear, she said, "Lewis, where ya gonna stick 'em?"

I whispered loudly in her ear, "In the butt!" The children burst out laughing and wanted me go with them in order to tell the adults that Doris Jean got some. "Y'all go ahead. I'm staying with Agnes and Doris Jean. Mama going to whup me. She gonna have to walk up here and whup my ass."

"Lewis, ya mama said give ya a message, you had better stop! She bouth ya in this world, she will take ya out!"

"Agnes, Mama was gonna kill A'Leous, so she can kill me. She fusing the hell outa me."

Agnes laughed and said, "Lewis, you had better stop cussing."

"Okay, Agnes."

"You better." (In 2012, my books will go viral with plays and film, and I have found the man for the character of A'Leous. I do not know his name, but he works in the shipping department factory in Charleston, South Carolina. As a child I said, "God made a beautiful man." As an adult I say, "God did not stop.")

Doris Jean was a smart baby. People talked around her not realizing she was a little tape recorder. People would say, "Don't tell Lewis. He will tell his mama." I would not voluntarily do so; she had to ask. Doris Jean knew this, and we had secrets. Mary Elizabeth (Libby), Aunt Carrie Lee's daughter said, "Lewis, Agnes want to see you." John Thomas (Woodchuck), Agnes, and Doris Jean were home. Doris Jean had on a sky blue gown and had hands together, like praying, and was looking down. Agnes was talking to me but watching Doris Jean.

"Lewis, I want you to tell me something. How do you know what happen, and you are not here. Tell me how you know so much?"

"Agnes, it's not hard to figure out. I figure it out by myself." Doris Jean smiled.

Agnes shouted, "Un huh, the cat is out the bag. It's Doris Jean!" We laughed. Agnes said, "Now it's two people we can't talk around here." My favorite cousin Mrs. Doris Jean Hollingsworth-Prince rest in peace, and I love you. Someday we will be together (Thank you, Ms. Diana Ross, The Supremes).

A poem called "Missing Children":

One is to many! Over two thousand a day, O God I pray. My great and powerful majesty, please God, end this travesty (65 percent are faceless and voiceless because of skin color).

Note: Mothers, safeguard your children, and fathers, protect your families. People took children then, now, and later. It's a shame so many children are missing. I propose making forever stamps since the five-year death rule ceased. The voice my beautiful mother heard was an act of God. The man she saw and heard no one else did.

"Carrie Lee, it was a dark skin man with beautiful white teeth. He wore a yellow plaid shirt and brown pants. When he was talking, he did not look at me. He was talking to the people setting close to the front door."

"Cille, no one 'member seeing that man. If I had a say, I will say that was your Guardian Angel!" Mama put her hands to her face. Rocking back and forth with tears flowing she said, "Thank you, Jesus."

Note: Thank you, Mr. Michael Baisden and Mr. George Welborn of the *Michael Baisden Radio Show* for bringing awareness of missing children to the airwaves.

Big Baby (Me)

Hollingsworth sisters [Lucille, Dorothy, Lily Mae,
Margarete, Carrie Lee, Bertrand Lewis (son)]

NOTABLE MENTIONS

Beau-friend said, "Lewis, staying home with ya, cause me to lose out on a lot of *poon-tang* (I did not know the meaning of the word, do not speak French). I told ya when I get clean as the board of health, I have to go to the club meeting. Didn't I tell ya the name of the club?"

"Yeah, you did. I 'member it's the Four F-ers."

"Lewis, you have a good memory when you try. I'm gonna give you a little history lesson on the one and only man's club. The Four F-ers all about women. Find the ladies, fool the ladies, fuck the ladies, and last forget (pause)."

I took the bait and said, "The ladies."

Beau-friend laughed, "That too, see I forgot already!"

"Beau-friend, when I get big, I'm gonna join your club."

Laughingly he said, "I'll keep a hole open for ya." He was talking over my head and enjoying the conversation. "Lewis, you are my brother. You'll not have to pay dues."

"I have to pay to be in this club?"

"You're cover. The new members have to pay. We have this money to take out the ladies. Once we finish with the ladies we all get stink fingers for the new members to smell."

"What! I have to pay money in order to smell fingers. Beau-friend, I change my mind."

"Lewis, it's gonna come a day when ya smell stink fingers. I know it's gonna be soon. I see bumps on your forehead." Beau-friend did not lie; puberty hit. I smelled a lot of stink fingers.

We were poor but rich in life. Two sisters and a brother did not stay close. Aunt Margaret H. Stewart lived on Price Street, same town (it appeared she did not like visitors, so she was not bothered much). Aunt Ester H. McCormick-Petty (passed away June 14, 2014) the baby, had always resided in Brooklyn, New York. Uncle Thomas Hollingsworth resided Wilmington, Delaware. The other sisters stayed reasonably close. We went to each other's houses often. The goings-on were not called a party. They were called "where ista happening or where ista goings-on?" The host would have a can too collect money. We would beg the host to cut out the bottom in order to see how much money was taken up. Money determined how hard you had to perform. You could win money for singing, dancing, tricks, jokes, anything entertaining for our parents to make them proud or laugh our troubles away.

Mr. Houston Goldston was the original old school player. He wore a derby (hat) with a long feather, a brown suit, highly shined tan shoes, and a cherry tree walking stick. He walked very slowly—heel to toe, lean that way, heel to toe, lean that way. "Mama, I think it's gonna take Mr. Houston Goldston two days to get home." He stayed one-half block away. Aunt Carrie Lee (Big Mama) cut out can bottom and dumped the contents in a handkerchief. O hell, somebody put a washer in the can. She matched up people with the money. Mr. Houston Goldston was the culprit.

"O baby, O baby, I gave ya the wrong coin. I'm sorry sweetheart. Honey, child, give me that back, baby. I gave ya the wrong coin." He took the small washer, gave her a larger one.

"Mr. Houston Goldston, what I'm gonna do with this washer?"

"Sweet thang, what letter in the center of that coin?"

"O!" said Aunt Carrie Lee.

"Well, what I'm saying, baby girl," he said, his finger pointing at his chest, "I-O." His finger was pointed at Aunt Carrie Lee, "U." The house went up with laughter. At each party we found a way to put a washer in the can, which we called the money jar. The host would say, "Hell, somebody put a washer in here." The response would be "I-O-U."

The party came back to Aunt Carrie Lee; as she opened the can, there were all washers. "What the hell I'm gonna do with all these washers?"

We all shouted, "I-O-U!"

"That's it! There will no more money jars. I want everybody to bring something. You don't have nothing, bring yourselves." We knew how to have fun and we did. (Remember or recall the singer Mr. Barry White? This is Mr. Houston Goldston with same size and the booming voice.) He said, "I am the roster in the henhouse." He called the old hens baby and the young tender thangs, baby girl. (In my favorite radio program, Ms. Dominique says "baby girl.") Mr. Keith Sweat, singer and disk jockey on the radio reminds me of the smooth talking Mr. Houston Goldston. He say "baby girl" on his show *The Sweat Hotel*. His show was for the ladies, so was Mr. Houston Goldston.

Mr. Ishmael Buf'fin was a man I admired and respected. Beau-friend told me how he came about. He was a small man who spoke many languages. French was primary. America is his newfound home. He volunteered to fight for America. The movie version of Mr. Audie Murphy (war hero) on a burning tank killing columns of Germans and not one ducked or took cover is far-fetched. Mr. Ishmael Buf'fin, war hero, called out to the enemy. Someone raised their head, he shot them between the eyes. Returning to Louisiana in uniform with many medals, he went to the trade store to buy gear for work, trapping. A fat white man walked up, tapped a medal on his chest, and said, "Boy, you git them there medals for killing white folks? We donna take it kindly around herah for niggers coming back herah with medals for killing white folks. One nigger was found hung in that big old oak tree at city hall. Those medals donna save his black ass. Another nigger in uniform, chest full of medals, driving a brand-new convertible caddylac (sic). ACME cement truck accidentally poured cement in the car. We believe that nigger was sleep inside." He just up and disappeared. Mr. Ishmael Buf'fin ran to his car. left turn signal kicking up dust he went right as the white men ran to their trucks. The trick worked. He decided that wherever the car stopped would be home. Eastbound, his car stopped on the outskirt of town. Two men helped him push the car in the bush. This would be home for now.

He made his way to the poolroom.

"Mr. John Robinson have keen eyes. Lewis, he notice the little man had game, a plan to get back money lost over the years. Lewis, the white man and the mulatto pool shark are coming Saturday. The poolroom will be packed, so come early, get in your hiding place under the bench, and don't come out. We have a secret weapon. The white man had a brown hat, Mr. John Robinson a blue hat. A dollar bet the white man match. Five dollars and above, you say your name and amount. It is written down. (The mulatto today would be Mr. Michael Ealy, actor, with the exception that his hair was curly brown with blond ends and green eyes, while filming Mr. Steve Harvey, protégé in *Think Like a Man*. A man of comedy, Mr. Kevin Hart, teases him about having the Incredible Hulk green eyes. He makes the correction, "My eyes are blue.") Before, I called him "the mulatto." Today I call him Mr. GQ (Gentleman Quarterly) because of his attire that complemented his green eyes. He wore tan shoes, green socks, shark skin suit (brown), green shirt, tie (brown-and-green), gold cuff links, green ring on pinkie finger, and a gold watch. He adored the attention on stage as all eyes would be on him, gleaming as he sized the competition. They appeared to be overconfident. The locals rendered he could beat blindfold.

"All bets down, let's began" said Mr. John Robinson. On cue, the men moved aside. Mr. Ishmael Buf'fin walked down, dressed in all black. He sported a black beret with a white ball on top. He opened his pool case and displayed a black ivory pool stick with a white end. First contest to decide who goes first was closer to the back rail break. Mr. GQ cue ball a half inch from the back rail. Mr. Ishmael Buf'fin cue ball touching the rail. I said, "Damn, I should had given Beau-friend money to bet."

"Lewis never be scare of your money, more where it came from." The poolroom were so quiet you could hear a pin drop. Mr. Bro Ditty Smith racked the balls and offered to Mr. GQ. He racked tighter. "Side bet for the players, each ball a dollar. Play the balls consecutively. Best three out of five games."

Mr. Ishmael Buf'fin played all the balls with the cue ball in position for the next game. Next game, same outcome, as Mr. John Robinson with his arms folded kept his composure; however, the men had a hard time controlling the enjoyment of winning. The men should have asked my brother about "scare of your money." Mr. Trick Knight summed it up for the men in the back. "If I had more, I woulda bet more. After all these years they been taken my money, it's a damn shame they come when I'm broke." Mr. Bro Ditty Smith racked the third game and offered the rack to Mr. GQ. He refused, and that was a big mistake. Mr. Ishmael Buf'fin played many balls on the break. The men looked at Mr. Bro Ditty Smith, grinning. "We caught you with your hands in the cookie jar." (Today it would be "You are guilty of this, you got blueberries all over your face." Thank you, Reverend Al Sharpton, "MSNBC.")

The men said, "That rack was so lose you could see daylight between the balls. They suppose too touch." Mr. GQ never got a shot with class; all eyes were on him. He did a reverse routine, except for taking the ring off his pinkie finger and the cuff links out of his pocket. He gave the items up. Looking down on the Frenchman, he said, "You are only good until you play the next man." He turned as the white man came from behind the counter and put his right arm on his right shoulder, talking to him. Mr. GQ was consoled by the white man. I imagine he said, "Do not let this get you down. We'll get them the next time," as they walked away. From the back, I noticed they resembled each other. I laid to rest father and son. The winners were loud, witnessing history and wanted to get a fat ass white man name Minnesota to play Mr. ISH (E-she).

Mr. John Robinson said, "Lower your voices," while distributing winnings. He could not hear himself think. "Nobody get shortchange, it may be you." The men became quiet.

Mr. Trick Knight said, "ISH (E-she), you should have played for the gold watch."

"E-fen-day (friend), ven (when) tou gotten ze mon (Mr.) down, das, ven tou kicka him inda ass. Ze watcha ista not importante, ze Ishmael Buf'fin, expresso, live and let liva."

The jubilation got to me, and I had to make a grand exit. I stood on the back bench and shouted, "Mr. ISH is the best!" I started walking out.

"Lewis, wait! Come here, what you say?"

"Mr. ISH is the best!"

Mr. John Robinson called on the poolroom official drum major Mr. Trick Knight. "ISH is the best, let's hear it!" The men are given the green light to act up. They did not disappoint. They laughed, chanted, and tossed Mr. ISH in the air carefully; he is a pint-sized man. Mr. JR, Doctor Simmons, and Beau-friend were not afraid of betting large amount of money. People said "they made a killing." The men lined up and put money in Mr. ISH's coat pocket; however, when Trick reached for his pocket, he said, "O contra ze trickster, ze puta hand in ze pocket nothing ista left zou puta moo-lah inda hand."

He drew back shouted, "O, no ISH! It's gonna be like that?" The men burst out laughing.

Someone said, "Trick Knight put his hand in my pocket. He's gonna pull back a nub!" Mr. John Robinson gave me two bags of peanuts and a grape soda.

"Mr. John Robinson, I know beggars should not be choosey, but somebody gave Genie Boy orange. May I please change it?" Looking at Beau-friend, I wondered who gave it to him.

"Lewis, take both."

"Thank you, Mr. John Robinson."

"You are welcome, Lewis." As Mr. JR turns he gives my brother a signal by pointing a hook finger. Beau Friend would say, "Lewis, take ya ass home!" The men were overjoyed. They started saying it.

"Hold it! Hold it! Only Beau-friend can say this. Lucille McLean and her sisters are not gonna kill me!"

Beau Friend said, "Lewis, where is Cille and Genie Boy?"

"They went to Aunt Carrie Lee to the catfish and cabbage wine party. Mr. Hayward Peoples gave the stuff, and she had to sack people up talking about they not gonna eat or drink. They don't know where he got it from. She said, 'That's more for me and the children 'cause as soon as that fish hit that hot grease belly full of cabbage wine and moonshine. Y'all be first in line after seeing Mr. Hayward Peoples fishing in the toilet hole.' I think she been sampling the wine not somebody be picking teeth off the floor, eating, drinking from a straw."

"Yeah, Lewis, did she say her motto?"

"Naw."

"Well, she's mellow with the wine or shine. What are ya doing home?"

"Trying to get *Randy's Record Mart* (radio program)."

"Go down the channel to the very end. You can get a better reception late at night. Planning to get something to play the records on?"

"Naw, just love music." Miz Sis Womack (Billy's mother) told Mama that I could come on Saturday mornings and listen to her records. "Yeah, Lewis, they are nice folks, and I heard she has a lot of records."

"You mean you heard it thru the grapevine, don't ya?"

"Lewis, a smart-ass is not ya cup of tea, so shut the hell up and listen. Mr. ISH got a challenge from some city slicker Saturday, ya coming?"

"What can stop me?"

"Mr. John Robinson can, stupid."

"Beau-friend, I say what not who."

"Keep been smart, Lewis. I'm gonna forget I told ya."

"You know you gonna forget you told me. That's funny, funny."

"You don't see me laughing, do ya? So I'll let Mr. John Robinson know you are sneaking in."

"Beau-friend, you are really confusing the hell outa me. Why ya telling him I'm sneaking in?"

"That's my job, stupid. Now shut up before I dust ya off."

"Well, I know when I'm not wanted."

"Going to the party, are ya coming?"

"Naw, I got a date. I can smell fish over there." He laughed like there was no tomorrow. "C-ya, Beau-friend."

"Not if I C-ya first. C-ya, Lewis."

The poolroom was filled to capacity. I could not sneak in. The outside door made a noise you could hear a mile away. Noise and no one appeared, Mr. John Robinson would look down the hallway. My prayer was answered; two painters were going in. I wondered how much paint was needed on the walls; it appeared they were wearing a couple gallons. I will not ridicule the men. They were working, not here hustling. I ducked in my hiding place. Mr. City Slicker had on a "Saturday Night Live" suit. It looked off-white; it was hard to tell. His mouth was full of gold and may have thrown off the shade a little bit. Mr. CS prejudged the Frenchman. He went to Mr. Bobby Martin, who was tall, light complexion and black wavy hair.

"Are you the Frenchman?"

"No, you just passed him."

Mr. CS turned back with a stupid "you got to be kidding" look on his face. A pint-sized black man, he said something. Mr. ISH let him have both gun barrels. I did not understand the language, but as he was pointing to the tall light-complexioned men with curly, wavy hair, I got his drift. The only way he could stop the onslaught: He took out a leather whiskey flask from the inside coat pocket and offered to Mr. ISH. They drank twice, hugged, and did a song-and-dance routine. Offered to Mr. JR. He refused. There was a money belt around his waist; he gave the contents to Mr. JR, who put it in a cigar box. Mr. JR let the men bet with him. Everyone were happy, as Mr. JR was willing to spread the wealth. Mr. CS flipped the coin and won. Someone suggested the coin should have been checked. He had game. I thought, "A reversal of Mr. GQ." I prayed that he should miss on every shot. Finally, the ten balls went around the pocket and came out. He checked the pocket and said, "Damn! I know too much English and not enough French." Well, sir, you need to learn French; you will be taught French. That was his last shot. For the final rack, he refused to tighten the balls. Mr. Bro Smith lived up to his name Do Wop Ditty, original one and only. The pool game was for thirty-five cents; give him fifty cents and say, "Rack 'em tight, Ditty" (hood talk: the key words are opposite), and the rack would be so loose you could hit the one ball with a marshmallow and balls would fall. Many balls went in, and the cue ball was heading for the corner pocket and it stopped on a thread. We were all praying. If it fell, chances were we would lose. "Kick a man when he's down" is the rule to live by, and Mr. CS had game. Mr. ISH made a miraculous shot, game over! They talked. Mr. CS left the poolroom, leaving his coat and tie. He returned with three beautiful ladies. Mr. ISH and the short dark lady left.

"Well, y'all, I'm gonna play cards, win some money back."

This was wishful thinking; as a kid, I knew the odds were three to one. The men playing were on the job. "Hey, y'all, I got two gold mines here and a silver mine upstairs. Anybody want to talk?" I'm all ears. They do what, when, where, and how, I tell 'em. Y'all shoot pool so my friends can see the wares. The locals were a tight-knit group, and no one wanted to be labeled as having to buy pussy when we could get it free; however, we know different. Nothing is free; everything comes with a price. This also was perceived as a sign of disrespect toward Mr. John Robinson, and I am sure if his wife, Mrs. Ella, was told that pussy sold in the poolroom, he would get a frying pan upside his head. (Mr. Henry Woodard came from New York City with a large sum of money. Three consecutive days and nights there was vigil gambling. Mrs. Ella showed up with the frying pan, demanding why he did not come home. Some men say she should have come earlier, bopped them with the frying pan, and stopped the madness. Mr. Henry Woodard left town with more than he came with.)

Mr. CS said, "I wish someone here would scream at me like they do in the city as they take ya moo-lah (money). Y'all are just too nice, but ya still take my moo-lah."

Mr. CS shouted, "Oh hell! The Frenchman have my silver mine hour and thirty-four. Someone show my ladies the Frenchman room. Tell her let's go or I'm coming up there with my belt."

The ladies returned talking in a high-pitched English and French combined language (Creole). "Oh hell! My lady done fell head over heel for the Frenchman. Tell her come down, we'll talk about it." The silver mine came talking a mile a minute. He turned his head, pointing at the door. "Get her in the car, or I'll take a belt to ya!"

I am sure my brother told Mr. JR that I was sneaking in; however, with the beautiful people showboating, I was forgotten. Mr. CS put on his attire, got to the door, and said, "Will someone tell the Frenchman if he wants to go I'll wait for him. Please tell Scotty (local band, Scotty and his Revue) about the eye candy (beautiful ladies) I brought down, and I'm sorry for his lost. Oh, I see y'all have not heard. They were to play at the Oddfellow Hall tonight. My ladies were to be rump shakers, but I got word some lowlife stole his drums. Can't have a band without drums."

All the men including me looked at Mr. Trick Knight, who made a great move. He looked behind him to see what we were looking at. The men would not say anything while Mr. CS there. A rule: "Do not air out your dirty clothes when you have company." The wrath of the poolroom would be on him once the company left. The runner told Mr. CS so all could hear. Mr. ISH said, "Go ahead, he's staying. This is where his friends reside."

"Well, I enjoyed the stay, but I hate y'all for taking my moo-lah (money) and smiling at me. You are all nice people, so long."

They hurried him off with the many "so longs" and "c-yas." They were beyond themselves waiting for the guest to leave so the dirty laundry could be aired. The first to be ridiculed was Mr. Tom Wilson, who had not won a big money game in five years. The nine ball in the pocket—all he had to do was touch it with the cue ball. He had lined up to shoot. The beautiful gold mine with the long hair was playing a shot. To get a better position, she put her right leg on the table. Mr. Tom Wilson looked up and missed the shot. People wanted to see him win a game in their lifetime; all eyes were on him. The men had to bite lips, and they pretended not seeing as they held back laughter. He was family, and you do not cut each other down when outsiders are around. Mr. Tom Wilson was light-skinned. He turned red and smiled. He was not totally silent as the men teased him. He had a great comeback for the men, which made them move to an easy prey, Mr. Trick Knight.

(Mr.) Topsy doing a play-by-play announcer with an imaginary microphone asked, "What happened?"

Leaning on the pool stick under his chin, Mr. Tom Wilson said, "I was blinded, but now I see." Men started drumming on the counter.

A man said, "Trick Knight, give the drummer some."

He screamed, "I didn't do it!"

A man shouted, "You hit a pig, he'll squeal."

Another said, "You hit a dog, he'll hollow."

All the men shouted, "Ya hit Trick Knight, he'll say!"

He screamed, "I didn't do it!" The laughter and dancing stopped.

Mr. John Robinson said, "This is the first time in my life I believe Trick didn't do it. No one saw him, and we know Scotty is looking for who did this."

Mr. Trick Knight said, "Y'all know Scotty don't play. He got that little gun with the big handle. He ain't shot nobody yet, but he have pistol whip a bunch'a niggers. I don't want to be on that list for somethang I didn't do."

Mr. JR said, "Hey, somebody go check on ISH, see when he's coming down."

A man said, "Trick, we know you have not been running 'cause of the name you got for honesty."

The men laughed and said, "Where ya get ze money, Ze Trickster?"

"Y'all some nosey niggers believing in kicking a man when he's down. There is two people here that won't kick ya. They'll give ya a hand. You got the white mouth (hungry). One man will feed ya. The other young man says business is good, and I know ya don't take handouts so I'll put this money in your pocket."

Mr. Charlie (Chicken) Floyd said, "Trick, stop the bullshit. Nobody around here do that shit." The men were using profanity openly. All right they did not know I am there.

"Well, Chicken, the day you walk in my shoes, need help, then ya will know. They, Chicken Floyd, means more than one and are good people."

Everyone knew he was talking about Mr. John Robinson (Godfather) and Beau-friend. Mr. Charlie (Chicken) Floyd wanted to downplay the moment. After his state-paid vacation (prison), the men did not reach out to him. Simply put, he had a caring family: Ms. Belle, Mr. Van, Ms. Dorema Williams (his mother living at the time), and other family members' support. Mr. Trick Knight only had the original "Wild Thang," Mr. Bobbie Knight, his brother. I was seeing the men in true form, meaning you got caught with your pants down. One man was the loudest. He made fun, and if you did not laugh, he would keep repeating the punch line tickling until you laughed. My friend, Mr. Bernard (Saint) Harris, was at his uncle Tan Harris's house. He saw him sneaking into his friend's back door as his friend left through the front door for work. Saint gave him the name "Back Door Wad-dale." "Back Door" is the short form. (In my writings, men doing negative things usually do not get the title of Mister. The only time I witnessed his activities, he was seriously looking in the eyes of his friend as the men teased him. He said, "A man can only go as far as the women let him." I bestow the title; he is called Mr. Back Door.) The poolroom became quiet. Men looked at the front entrance, grinning. It was the moment of truth; walking slowly with a smile was the man of the hour, Mr. Ishmael Buf'fin, dressed in black with something around his neck, black with yellow design—an ascot. (A famous journalist and commentator wears this attire today, Mr. Roland Martin. Mr. ISH (E-she) would be proud that someone carried on this classy tradition.) I upgraded the exit speech by Mr. GQ. "You are only good until you play the next (man) person." Now it's a kick-ass game with ladies holding their own. In my eyes, the best of the best wore black—Mr. Ishmael Buf'fin and a very beautiful lady, Ms. Jennifer Lee, called the Black Widow. Mr. Back Door broke the silence.

"ISH (E-she), ya the man! I had your hands. I'll cut mines off! ISH. don't worry bot them, just give me the secret! That gal was throwing in the towel and crying in a bucket. She says I'm staying with ISH, so fuck it! ISH, that gal was in love. What ya do, ISH? Let the world know! Mon (My) e-fen-daze (friend), ISH de firsta (first) tou (too) give va ze madam enda ze lifes, Ze-woo lah-lah."

The men knew what he meant; I did not have a clue.

"Mon (Mr.) Robinson, ze walls damage ze was climbing ze walls as ISH, Ze—woo lah-lah."

The men were laughing, except Mr. Charlie (Chicken) Floyd, who was sad-faced. He could not get over the treatment he had received compared to Mr. Trick Knight. He took the rap while everyone else walked freely away. The blessing of the men should have been on him; he had earned it. I think he lost out, coming back telling people they owed him. He was very talkative and forgot or just disregarded the slogan: "What happens in prison stays in prison." (Today, this concept has been given to Sin City.) Men went on the state-paid vacation (prison), and you would not know it. Some for petty crimes such as looking at a beautiful white lady as she bent over to retrieve something. A forty-pound ball was chained to the foot of some men while in prison. After leaving prison the men walked liked they were still carrying the forty pound ball. He even said, "Trick was a girl in prison." The men distanced themselves from him. Many said, "Prison ruin my life." He said that about Trick, "Maybe he heard the devious things I did in prison and revealed to Lord who knows." The men lived by the law of the poolroom: "When a man down, that's when you kick him."

Mr. Back Door waited for the chatter and laughter to die down. Looking at the downed man, he stood and shouted, "Chicken Floyd! You are a woo lah-lah motherfucker!" The poolroom erupted with laughter. The ice broken, he snapped out of it, laughing. I laughed loudly.

Mr. JR said, "Hold it! Hold it! It's a quiet mice in the house." Fingers pointed toward Beau-friend. "Lewis, take ya ass home!"

Some men say, "Lewis not here." Most of the time I was early and they would see my feet in the hideout. The men had let their guard down. Some men still said, "Lewis not here."

I jumped up, threw my hands out palms facing up, and shouted, "Ze-woo lah-lah!" The response was deafening. Even Mr. ISH was out of control with laughter. Mr. JR unfolded his arms and motioned to me.

"Lewis, you cannot leave empty-handed. Grape soda, right?" I liked grape, but my brother liked orange. Looking at Beau-friend, I wondered who gave him that orange soda. "Take both."

"Thank you, Mr. John Robinson." I hurried for the exit and turned with a bow, with the thumb and fingers touching. Putting my hand to the mouth and blowing a kiss, I said, "Ze-woo-lah-lah!" The men laugh at my innocence, stupidity, or both. I did not know what this meant. I did see the result firsthand. I do recall a man near my hideout saying, "ISH, Woo-lah-lah that shit. He done suck every dick north of the Mason Dixon line."

I was home, listening to the radio, searching for new materials for our show time, because children were the party entertainers. People would say back in the day I could do that. A man said, "Lewis, do that one leg dance with the pushup, then the split. Man, I could do that dance until I broke my back in the Army."

"Yeah man, I didn't know why Miz Mary Durham saw you coming and said, 'Drink up, here comes that freeloader old broke back.' You walked in. Yelled, 'I broke my back in the army and waiting on my check for the last five years. Only if I was white I would have my money and not owe every Tom, Dick, and Harry.'"

The name of the drink or the main course determine the name of the party. Beau-friend came into the house. "Lewis, where is Cille?"

"She's at Aunt Dorothy for the liver pudding hog skin party." Liver pudding was ground portions of the hog not wasted. The only thing not eaten was the "oink, oink." The hog skin was placed in the oven and cooked all night. Next morning, everyone had a Crisco can, and the grease was shared. You cooked or put that *shigidy* (word coined by Mr. Ken Smuckley, mother) in everything. Today, pork skin is a multi-million-dollar operation, by which, it was considered not useful in my childhood and given to Negroes. One thing that have not been successful—stolen vinegar pork rinds. Jews were a common fixture in the hood, who observed and took advantage of any monetary endeavors. After watching Negroes pour Penrose sausage juice in the pork rind bags, it was tried. A complete failure, very nasty. They used the Penrose chemical juice Mama used, blah zay, blah zay (I will not reveal. This will be my venture, and I do not want it stolen like my concept of "park and ride"). They have a dry powder salt and vinegar product today, which is also very nasty.

"Beau-friend, what are you doing home early?"

"Mr. John Robinson have a plan. Trick can get some work, he come early, I come later. Also school him on honesty. When a man say keep the change, is it enough? Always say yes. Put the money in the bag or your hand. Only put in the pocket after given and learn to say thanks."

"You think he got the drift?"

"Yeah, Lewis, this is his last chance and rather let himself down before Mr. John Robinson. When ya left, Charlie Floyd did what he should have from the beginning, shut up! Mr. John Robinson hugged him and put a wad of money in his pocket. The men did the same, except Trick. He was sitting on the bench with all eyes on him. He did not look behind like before. This is man-up time, prove you are the better man. Trick took two dollars out of his pocket and unfolded, so everyone could see. Put the money in Floyd pocket without bringing nothing out, and turn to walk away. Floyd

65

grab him, and they hugged. I think this is when Mr. John Robinson decide to give him another chance. He put a wad in Floyd pocket. He's rich. Trick put two dollars. Who gave the most?"

"I'll say Mr. John Robinson, unless that was a fake knot, and I know he do not roll like that. He's a good man."

"Nice try, Lewis, ya are wrong as usually. 'Member I say he is rich, he has more. Trick put more. That was all he had."

"It's a story like this in the Bible."

Whoa! I am not giving him another talent religion. Beau-friend's conversations made me walk off five paces, and do the sign of the cross.

"Lewis, I'm talking to ya. Why ya walking away?"

"One word, 'lightning bolt.'"

"Stupid, 'lightning bolt' is two words."

"Not in your case, mister."

He would catch me still swearing. "When I go, you are going with me! I'm praying, so we will go to different places." We laughed.

"Hey, Lewis, let's get to the fun stuff sinning, and grinning. You remember (Mr.) Tom Wilson missing the big money ball when the lady put her leg on the table?"

"Yup!"

"Your hideout is right there. When she put her leg on the table, did you see anything?"

"Yup!"

"Well, what did you see?"

"Beau-friend, I don't know, but it sho was damn ugly!" He started screaming and crying. He was scaring the hell out of me. "I would say, Beau-friend, it sho was damn ugly," and he started over.

Finally, "Lewis, stop! I have something important. You do not know what it is. You know what it look like?"

"Yup, a little man with a bald hook head. Beau-friend, he sho was damn ugly!"

"That's it, Lewis, get out now! It's a damn shame."

"Why? It sho was damn ugly? Naw, you are kicking me out of my own room. C-ya, Beau-friend."

"Not if I c-ya first, c-ya, Lewis."

The next day, Mama was acting strange. She wore her feelings on her sleeve. I needed to get out of Dodge (Dodge City) before she cornered me. "Mama, going to Aunt Dorothy, watch *Sea Hunt* (television program)."

"Come here, Lewis. I don't want to hear tell you ever going in the poolroom again. That's not a place for children, you hear me?"

"Okay, Mama."

"Don't try me. I'm serious, Lewis!"

"Okay, Mama."

"When you old enough to go then go, now you just a child, and I say again no place for you."

"Okay, Mama. You not gonna throw a shoe at me?"

"You go in there again, I'm not gonna throw shoes. I'm throwing bricks at your head, and my bricking is out of practice. So I'm telling you sorry now, just in case your head stop a few, ya listening?"

"Naw, Mama, I'm hearing!"

"Lewis, the poolroom keep asking about ya."

"Tell 'em somebody told Mama, and I'm not allowed to go back. If I find out who told, I'm throwing bricks at the head, and my bricking not that good. Beau-friend, you know I'll not go against Mama words."

"I know, Lewis. Between us, Mama finding out did not come from the poolroom. The poolroom is family. Mr. John Robinson would have somebody head, banded from the poolroom and maybe ran out of town if it came from the family. Lewis, I think the guilty party is talking now."

"What! You think Mama slip back from the party and was listening?"

"Naw, I think she slip back and was hearing outside your window. She knew you was home alone so she slip back to check on ya and got an earful. (Parents, you have my blessing, check on your children. Expect the unexpected. Have a course of actions, bricks at the head is old school. Control assets: the car, computers, cell phones, electronic gadgets, family time; it will bring positive results. It's okay to check rooms in your house; if justification is warranted, just say "I am from the show me state Missouri.") I told them about the 'sho was damn ugly,' and they laughed. Wad'dale said he would give his left nut to hear you say it."

"Well, I don't know. I overheard some men say Wad'dale is ball-less, so it might not be worth getting kill by Mama. Sho ya right! Beaufriend, I think we should check the next time we have something important to talk about."

"Yeah, I know."

"Lewis, turn the radio down before ya go deaf!"

"Huh, Mama, what ya say!"

She laughed and said, "You not doing something. Come help in the kitchen. A real man knows his way around the house. Your wife get mad and say, 'I'm not cooking.' Tell her, 'Okay, I don't need ya.'" (Many years later, I was stationed at Fort Bragg, North Carolina. My wife (Hyon Sun Pak) had driver's license for two weeks. She wanted to take her girlfriends in the snow to the bingo parlor in my brand-new car. "Tell your girlfriends get their husbands cars and go." "No!" "Then why are you playing me stupid!" "Dad, I'm not going to cook!" My four-year-old daughter Angie looked at me wide-eyed. "Mom don't cook, we don't eat!" The expression on her face depicted "What are we going to do?" "Don't worry, sweetheart, I got this!" I drove the car in the snow. Why, I was stupid to prove a point given to me by my beautiful mother at an early age. I got fresh vegetables at the commissary (army grocery store) and asked the butcher, "Would five dollars get me the colonel cut?" A soldier's saying: "Officers get top brand, we got generic foods." Her girlfriends came to the house. I made a large pot of beef stew. My daughter was surprised and happy. "Dad, I did not know you can cook." "I learn from my mother, and she would say, 'A real man knows his way around the house.' I'll explain to you when you get older, okay?" "Okay, Dad, can I have another bowl please?" "Sure, sweetheart." Her girlfriends started coming for bowls and said, "It's delicious." "Dad, you fix everybody food except mine, why?" "Honey, I don't need ya!" "Angie, tell Dad to fix mine please." "Okay, Dad fix Mom bowl please." "Okay, Angie." It was the only time over thirty-five years she said, "I'm not going to cook." It was the only time over thirty-five years I said, "I don't need ya.")

Mr. Van Williams, Ms. Frankie Alston (daughter of high school teacher, Mrs. Alston), Mr. Doyle Turner, and others went to the white library at late night. The librarian would not look up when they entered. Someone told the city manager, "Black niggers are using the library at night." The city manager watched as Negroes went in the library.

Approaching the librarian, he said, "You know niggers are in here!"

"No way, sir! They had to enter when my head was down." Posted signs about silence and disturbing others were ignored. "Niggahs! You niggahs get out! You are not welcome here! You are not allow on the premises. Leave before I call the police!" The next day she went to her friend, Mrs. Alston's house. She wanted to tell the children in person that she was sorry, and she did this to save her job. She had a plan to make it up to the students. The old books and excess books which she would order (two more would be sent), she would not annotate on the inventory and build a library for the students. She bypassed her racist boss and took the plan to Mayor Fields. He liked her plan. She told her friend that the mayor had a crush on her since school days. She was an attractive lady. He even let her rent the closet building on Wall Street for a dollar a year from the city. As Mr. Simpson White, me, and other kids started putting books on the truck, the racist city manager walked up, screaming, "What are you doing! These things are to be burned up! Why are these niggers putting books on the truck? You had better stop them! Who idea to give these niggers anything!"

"Mr. City Manager, sir," Mayor Fields said, "you overstep your bounds. The law states separate but equal."

He says, "How can nothing be separate but equal?"

"These people will have a library, or they can use ours until they get one. Give you this letter describing what I said. Give them materials that will not hindrance our operations, or by proclamation they will be allow to use our library at a specific hour."

The racist city manager stormed away, saying, "The damn niggers are taking over. A damn library for what? Everybody knows. Niggers can't read or write!"

When the racist city manager ranted with the name calling, I watched Mr. Simpson White's left jaw. Bumps appeared as he clenched his teeth very, very tight.

A firsthand witness is a story worth telling. The word spread thoughout the hood like wildfire. "Something happen at Bland's Drugstore." I went to investigate. My thoughts were "Somebody have been kill at the railroad crossing. Mr. Bama Thompson, Mrs. Willie Mae Alston (Mr. Pal's wife), and others have been kill there, trying to beat the train." (Recently on my way to the Durham Veterans Affairs Hospital, an apparatus invented by a Negro was finally installed, drop gate. I will put black crosses in remembrance of people who have perished. No white person had been killed at this site.). When I got there, men were crying and wallowing on the ground. The only man with composure was Mr. Droopy Martin. "Droop, what happen?"

"We have been churching up (beg change from people entering, exiting the drugstore) all morning to get a gallon of wine. De'berry got it. Came out profiling and strutting like he's on the streets of New York City and drop the damn thang."

I ran home, got money from my money drawer, and slipped to Droop. Mr. Droopy Martin came out with the wine, holding it to his chest like carrying a baby and walking gently. The tears turned to cheers. "Droop, ya are the man. You was holding back on us. You wanna see grown men cry? We love ya, Droop." Before he acknowledged me, I made eye contact and shook my head no. This kind act could be detrimental to my health. Mama practiced throwing shoes; this warranted brick throwing, by which she did not practice. But she'd acknowledge her aim is off and tell you sorry in advance. Fifty-fifty chance Mama would say, "Lewis is free-hearted." I would not try her. She would probably say, "Lewis, these are able-body men, could work if they wanted to. You are getting a beat down, no excuse." In this situation, I will use her phases. "Leave well enough alone" and what she did not know could not hurt her. It was only fitting that the men on the Fair Promise AME Zion church ground sang church songs. A ritual that still occurs today is pouring wine out after opening. This is called getting rid of the poison. Also show respect for the brothers and sisters who died. The men let Mr. De'berry Sutherland go first. This jester to show no hard feeling and to identify his cup. No one would drink from his cup. He is a squatting man who wore the badge of fucking Little Richard proudly. The saying of the day was "a man that plug a butt hole will suck a pole and Dee got some mighty fine pussy lips. (Prison ruined my life.) The songs were beautiful. They harmonized "How Great Thy Art." People stopped and listened. Some men were in a crying mood as they sang. As usual, I had to come up with a name for the group. I never revealed the name of the group until now. I called them "Mr. De'berry and A Crying Shame." I thought, "Robert McLean will not let this talent be squandered. I will take this to a man of God, Reb J. R. Hampton."

"Reb Hampton, we can have the men here on communion." He laughed a long time.

Finally he said, "Robert, I like your idea, but it will be a problem in the church."

"Why?"

"The members will not accept them because they are winos. No, Robert, Mr. J. R. McIver and the deacons fight over the wine already."

"Sir, the deacons will not settle for holy water."

"Robert, not at Blandonia Presbyterian Church." We laughed. The mood was too surreal. The men cry when sad, cry when happy. The greatest fear was somebody might tell Mama I am hanging out with the winos. I moved to the opposite side of the building where the children were gathered. Mr. Simpson White drove up.

"Y'all doing anything?"

"No, sir!"

"Well, get on the back of the truck and do something. It will benefit you." One kid disrespected Mr. Simpson White by asking, "How much we gonna get paid?" After hearing this, we all got on the truck except the money-hungry kid. We gave him the look, yes the look: "You get on this truck, we will tell him to go fast, then we will throw your ass off."

He got the vibes. "Y'all go head. I got to go home anyway, c-ya." He did not get the normal response.

I said, "Yeah, we will see you when we get back, asshole!"

Mr. Simpson White was a successful man with a beautiful home and family. Yet in the eyes of the racist city manager he was just a nigger who could not read or write. Once we got back to our library, he offered thanks and money. All eyes were on me; I gave the look, yes the look: "You put your hand out, you going to pull back a nub." "Mr. Simpson White, we cannot accept money for something that's going to benefit us. Sir, why are we not putting the books up on the shelves?"

"Well, my wife wants to add her touch. She is the librarian." We gave him the look, yes the look: "Slap me, I'm stupid."

He said, "I'm not henpeck, I just got henhouse ways." We laughed and came to the conclusion Mr. Simpson White was all right. He shouted, "Let's do this!" I am sure he got off the hook by telling his wife, we forced his hand and he could not lose face. I kept books past due. She would reprimand with a beautiful smile.

The libraries met state law standards—separate but equal. One was a two-story building with wall-to-wall books. In the other one, the librarian had the first wall-to-wall desk. On opening day, I am floored; Mr. Simpson White had a beautiful wife, and I came to the conclusion, a librarian's qualification you have to be beautiful. The school librarian was also beautiful, Mrs. Ruby Maxwell. The White's had twin daughters. My favorite teacher Mr. Lloyd Hoover married one. What was special about the twins? They did not shave their legs.

The library opened at 10:00 a.m. On the way. I met a shell of a man with boots not laced, white long socks, olive green shorts with pockets, T-shirt without sleeves (call wife beaters the garment worn by Ike, when he beat Mrs. Tina Turner), gray wool blanket draped over his shoulders, no beret, eyes straight ahead, and walking slowly. I ran to the poolroom. I lost touch, of Mama's warning I adhered to. I waited for someone to come out. "Bro'Ditty Smith, will ya please tell Beau-friend to come out? It's an emergency!"

"What's wrong? Mr. Ishmael Buf'fin, what wrong with him! Oh shit! Lewis, ya scare the hell outa me. He's fighting the war. He killed a lot of people. They are haunting him, and he can't sleep. He's walking around for the last time 'cause Mr. John Robinson got him some help. People are coming to get him today. When! I don't know."

"Well, I'm waiting!"

"Not here. You know Mama got eyes everywhere when it comes to you. Naw, Wall Street Baptist Church steps. Ya not going to the library?"

"Not today. This is too important."

"Okay, get over there and watch the cars."

"Okay, c-ya, Beau-friend."

"C-ya, Lewis." He let me off the hook; the second person says, "Not if I see ya first." He knew I respected, loved the way Mr. ISH dressed, acted, talked, and played pool. The smart aleck remark did not hold water. To all his many talents, now I add psychology. I sat and waited until a white-and-yellow ambulance turned into the parking lot. Two giants dressed in white took the gurney inside. A short time later, Mr. John Robinson and the family came out to bid farewell to Mr. Ishmael Buf'fin. He resembled a child in bed.

I stood on the top step and shouted, "Mr. ISH is the best! Mr. ISH is the best!"

Mr. John Robinson said, "Who is that?"

"That's Lewis! That's my brother." I went down Foster Alley, crying.

He was a great man, an immigrant fighting for America so conservatives cowards could stay and protect the women and children. He killed Nazis, Fascists, Socialists, and enemies of America in order to be downplayed as killing white people. He was not an Algerian Frenchman. He was a true American. (Conservatism should be defined. People serve in the armed forces or instill your own children to serve. (Mr. Charles Rangel Lawmaker was censured. He said, "We have the draft. We will not fight unnecessary wars. It's hard for lawmakers to send their own in battle, yet easy to put other people's children and loved ones in harm's way.") Conserve your principles beyond the shores of America. Fight the enemies foreign or domestic (even in the halls of Congress), white or indifferent. Conserve a way of life which provides programs to adjust after tours of duty and jobs. I pray, dear God, we will build a shelter for returning homeless veterans or anyone who need a place to rest their head, Amen.)

Beside the Masonic Hall on Odd fellow Street, men were throwing horseshoes. Mr. Hoskin Thompson, the best player of all times said, "Hey you know how to pitch horseshoes?" I shook my head no. "Well, stop that crying. Get over here. You are my partner."

On my first throw, the shoe rolled, and the men shouted, "Whoa, mule!" "Whoa, mule!" I laughed like there was no tomorrow and completely forgot the previous encounter. The men held back. We won five games and I was happy as a pig in slop. Mr. Hoskin Thompson said, "See the men here. This game is not for men only. Everyone can play. You prove that. You caught on fast so tell your mamas (Wow, it was written on my face hood rats do not have fathers) let the children come over. We don't cuss. Keep you out of the poolroom (Mama spread the word), and off the streets." He stayed across the road and would leave the equipment on the porch for us. We played all day, and the men came after it cooled down. We became proficient, and Mr. Benny Lee Smith concocted a plan. He said, "Our best players will always match up to the men with skills. If your team is beating our best players, Mr. Thompson or Mr. Snap Moore are next. You play to lose so our best would sat the men down." I hate listing. Someone left out would remind me in detail what they did at the family reunion. The title of "Mister" was warranted: Lawrence (birdman) McLaughlin, William (fatso) Hollingsworth, John (woodchuck) Hollingsworth, Bro Ditty Smith (left hand, half turn, a beautiful throw), Joseph (JT) Smith, Junior Smith, Bel'van (mellow yellow) Smith, Benny Lee Smith), Haywood (nen'nie) Hollingsworth, Calvin (Juice) McLean—think he's good now, my brother, I love and respect—and the children who came out to beat the men playing horseshoes. Mr. Snap Moore talked a great game and paid us to say he taught us everything he knew about the game. He shouted, "everyone gets a dime!" He gave a nickel and waited for the response. We played back what he said. "Well, a dime is a nickel twice, a nickel now the other one when you are nice!" We gave him the look, yes the look: "You not going to tell us it's raining and think we are not looking up, knowing you are pissing on our heads." He looked at us and laughed like there was no tomorrow.

On the day of reckoning Mr. Hoskin Thompson said, "We have created some horseshoe monsters. These children can play."

Mr. Snap Moore said, "I taught them everything I know."

Mr. John Willie Hamer said, "Snap, we know how much ya know, and these children are much smarter than that." Everyone laughed.

"Y'all don't believe me? Just ask them."

Mr. Charles Woodard said, "Did Snap teach y'all everythang he knows?"

We shouted, "Yes, sir!"

"Did he pay y'all to say this?"

"Yes, sir!"

Finally, "How much?"

In unison, we answered, "A dime is a nickel twice, a nickel now the other one when ya are nice!" The men roared with laughter. There was a house near the site; my uncle Mr. Charlie Blue and aunt Meany lived there and sold spirits. Respect went both ways. Some men would disappear. When returning, they became cheerleaders and ridiculed the men that lost.

Mr. Richard Hamer said, "Snap is such a cheapstake!" "I'm giving y'all the other nickel. The truth will set ya free." Afterward, he asked, "Did Snap Moore teach y'all everythang he knows?"

"No, sir!"

Mr. Snap Moore said, "Well, I agree I don't know a lot, but it's two thangs I do. These children can play horseshoes, and ya can pay them to say anythang. History will be made today. Me and Hoskin have never played together, but we have to teach the children a lesson they will never forget."

A short time later, the All-Star Team went to the loser's bench and whispered, "Slide down." The men would not let Mr. Snap Moore off that easy. "What ya say, Snap! Be careful, don't get splinters in your butt!" We took no prisoners.

Mr. Hoskin Thompson said, "Men, in order to beat the children, we have to come out earlier and warm up." On the loser's bench, you slide down to the end. We watched the bench in order to size up the competition and stay true to our plan. From the end of the bench, Mr. Hoskin Thompson looked up. Pointing, he said, "Those are some beautiful birds." I looked up and saw seven blackbirds or pigeons hovering. He was Looking up and pointing and saliva was drooling from the left side of his mouth. The men realized he was in trouble and took him into the house. For the first time an emergency vehicle came on Oddfellow Street to aid a Negro!

Mr. Snap Moore said, "Take the stuff. Y'all can make a site anywhere xcept here for the sake of his wife." Mr. Hoskin Thompson had a stroke and died. A great man who introduced us to a simple game of horseshoes. The game brought young boys and mature men together in harmony. (God willing, our shelter will have a horseshoe site called Mr. Hoskin Thompson, Mr. Snap Moore.)

We founded a site. While moving a board, I was attacked by hornets. My face on fire, I was screaming and crying like a newborn getting smacked by my midwife. (Ms. Sarah James, Leroy (Skeet) James's grandmother, who stayed on Washington Avenue, delivered Robert Lewis McLean legally through the womb). Doctors and hospitals were not for Negroes. (Today, my grandson Beau says, "My papa say I'm going to be a baby doctor, you know, a petertrition (sic)." He's three years old.) There was a home remedy for bee stings to stop swelling, pain, and make the stinger's surface—tobacco juice (saliva). The hood were at the house. I had to perform. Aunt Dorothy put the saliva on my face. I kept moving backward.

Mama said, "Lewis, quit moving back. It hurts?"

"Yeah, Mama!"

"What hurt?"

"Aunt Dorothy putting this spit on me, and I can't do a damn thang about it!" Mama and the hood laughed.

"Lewis, don't think ya gonna get away with this. I'm gonna whup ya."

"Aunt Carrie Lee (Big Mama), would ya tell Mama to whup me now while I'm in pain?"

"Lewis, I want ya to feel better. Than I'm gonna whup ya."

I had to get on the good side of my sweet Aunt Dorothy. She had clout—the only television. She had two good children and a mean one, who would hurt your feelings. "Go home and watch ya own television." My mean childhood cousin sweated on his nose (all year long), ate spoonfuls of mayonnaise out the jar, and loved to fight. His name is Mr. John T. Hollingsworth. I Love ya man!

"Aunt Dorothy, thanks for spitting on me."

"You are so welcome, Lewis. Call me anytime to spit on ya and that will be five dollars for the office visit."

"Oh Lord!"

"Lewis, you swear, I'm gonna whup ya for real."

"Thanks, Aunt Dot."

"You're welcome, Lewis."

"I'm going to bed while I can. C-y'all."

The hood shouted, "Not if we c-ya first! C-ya, Lewis."

"Lewis, came to check on ya. Looking at ya face, you got more kills than Mr. ISH. The hornets die after they sting ya."

"Well. I feel like joining them, but I promised I will keep my ass out of hell, 'member?"

"Yeah, I remember. They gave ISH a shot to make him sleep but he heard ya, 'cause he smiled. Beau-friend. I heard Mr. John Robinson say, 'Who's that?'"

"'They forgot me already!'"

"Don't sweat it. I'm at the poolroom every day, and they pretend not knowing my name. I get a lot of 'hey you.' I don't mind. I'm making money, and they can call me anythang except late for supper." We laughed. "You not gonna believe this. I'm the only kid in the hood that got sack by Aunt Dot. She usta let me get away saying things. She does not like hurting your feelings. Just mention around Woodchuck, then ya have a fight on your hand." (Then-children fought (pushing), argued, break up to make up, continued to play. Now-children use guns, knives, and boards to beat the brains out of a child, kill each other; children play stop!) God Bless the children! Agnes was close. I think she was in on it.

"Lewis, I heard."

"Oh man, already! Remember it was a lot of people here and you are the first to get sack by Dot."

"Well, I'm glad it was me. Kids gonna say she sack Lewis. I know I'm not gonna be next." She was the sweetest flower, my Aunt Dorothy Hollingsworth McLean, and a good man her husband, Mr. Alonzo McLean.

"Lewis, it's no more Trick Knight."

Mr. John Robinson said, "He's to be call Gene Knight."

Mr. Glenn Snipes said he did not like the new guy. "The old Trick, you expected to be rob. I heard he was looking for me, and I hid out for three weeks. He cornered me at Fleming Cafe and gave me thirty-five cents. 'Why you didn't just keep it?' 'It's not mine!' I told him to keep it, and I gave him a nickel more."

The men started shouting, "Here's a nickel more!" Putting money in Gene Knight's pocket, they laughed and welcomed the new family member. (Prelude of police beating Mr. Gene Knight.) Old black Mac's (black policeman) flunky came and waited for Mr. Gene Knight to leave on an errand. His name was Ed Dixon (the title mister is not warranted). He pretended to be asleep at the bus station, watching in order to keep the police informed on who was coming or leaving town. Hood talk: the keyword is opposite. He was called by everyone, including my mother, "Sleeping Beauty." He became bold and not caring what people would say. His mindset he was the police without a badge. Afterward, people called him, including my mother beauty.

"Lewis, Sleeping Beauty just happen to hear why old black Mac beat Gene Knight. Juanita, his girlfriend, is a married woman. Since her husband Joe is a kind-hearted man and not violent, he will send a message to the back door men. 'Mess with a married woman, you will be beat.'" This did not hold water. Sleeping Beauty was a back door man with a free pass. Gene was just accepted in the family. Mr. John Robinson turned his back to Sleeping Beauty, and we all did the same.

A traditional place where black men could assemble and discuss events entirely without fear of being beat or kill was the barbershop. The men were called Jack Legs (experts on life/the character (Eddie) Mr. Cedric the entertainer played in the movie *Barbershop* display this zeal). A remarkable man, Mr. Richard McIver was called the *Herald*, not because he walked around with a newspaper under his left armpit. Beau-friend said he had a photographic memory. He would close his eyes, tell you what happened in the news, and could go back seven days. The service was not free. You paid him a nickel, and if he was wrong, he would give you the same nickel back (never wrong in my childhood). A tradition faded with integration was the poolroom. This was a place black men could unwind and be themselves. They had wholesome fun, humor, and let it all hang out. Entertainment I borrowed a word from the British top-notch were conducted at the Masonic Hall on Oddfellow Street. Negroes went to mingle, court, watch plays (called revues). Little Richard was famous with the men. We loved a band from Fayetteville North Carolina, called Chocolate Buttermilk. A revue featured the thirteen wonders of the world. She broke men's hearts, wallets, and homes. She was called a war baby German and Negro. Her name is Ms. La'sue. Junior Smith found a crawl space. Spread the word. "If ya can keep a secret, sneak out, come and see Ms. La'sue shake that thang." I got there.

"Hell, we can't do this. Lewis is here, and he will tell his mama."

"Junior, I'll tell if she ask. That mean somebody have a big mouth and told first."

"Damn! Lewis, right, let's do this!" We crawled under this old wooden building infested with snakes, spiders, rats, and things we could not see in the dark. Ms. La'sue was shaking that thang to the east, to the west, to the men with money she loved the best. Mr. Billie Marsh went ape shit crazy. Threw dollars at her feet, squatted, kicked his feet out (Russian dance), jumped down, humped the floor. We burst out laughing.

"Hey, y'all, I hear voices! It's coming from the floor!"

"Billie, you are drunk! Pretty soon ya gonna tell us ya see thangs. Go sit down so the blood will go back to the big head." He would not let it go. Next day, he found the crawl space and told Mr. W. T. Horton, the undertaker and overseer of the hall. He had it boarded up. The next two weeks we walked around with a big smile on our faces. Mama and the Mothers of Gossip were on the porch, Ms. Alma White (her friend), Aunt Carrie Lee, and Aunt Dorothy. Mr. Junior Smith walked by; we made eye contact and started grinning.

Mama said, "Y'all notice the children seems so happy like they know something we don't. Lewis! Lewis, come here a minute."

"Oh Lord! What I'm gonna do?" My prayer was answered in a heartbeat. "Hey, y'all. Junior, come here. They not gonna believe this! We got dress down on a Saturday night. Crawl down under the Oddfellow Hall like we own it. People moved as we crawled our way to the front to watch Ms. La'sue shake that thang. Y'all watch me now! Oh y'ell, shake that thang! It must be jelly 'cause jam don't shake like that!"

"Lewis, stop! You are killing us!"

"Aunt Carrie Lee, watch this." A nasty gyrating move.

Mama screamed, "Lewis, you better stop!"

Mr. Junior Smith said as we walked away, "Damn, Lewis, you told them."

"Man, I have never lied to Mama. I ask God for help, and you know, he's an on-time deliver. Reasoning, Mama have never whup my ass while laughing. Wait, I forgot something. Aunt Dot, the dance cost you five dollars."

"Okay, Lewis, we are now even, but I'll spit on ya for free."

"Oh Lord, again."

"Lewis, ya better git while the git is good."

"C-y'all."

"Not if we c-ya first, c-ya, Lewis."

"Junior, go ahead. I don't feel like throwing at pigeons today. I'm going home and go to bed."

"You sick?"

"Naw, man. Mama say I have thin skin. Little things bother me."

"Okay, c-ya, Lewis."

"Not if I c-ya first, c-ya, Junior."

"Lewis, where ya going?"

"Home, Mama."

"Why ya not going to Aunt Ethel Smith and play with the children?"

"I'm going to bed while I can."

"You sick!"

"Mama, y'all sack me up so much today, I'm going home and sack out." (No comeback, wow I got them. I cannot make them aware that I sacked them. Mothers are off limit. (Disrespectful toward mothers, any adult in the hood, have a green light to beat your ass if you ever have the nerve to get smart with your mother.)

Aunt Carrie Lee laughed and said, "That Lewis is a mess!"

"Un huh and some said Mama." The Ladies Of Gossip, I love y'all forever.

The overseer shouted, "Y'all niggahs better learn fast, or I'll killya all!" (Pillage from *Roots*.) Livestock were treated better than the captured people. Customs, languages, manhood, womanhood, and well-being were destroyed. Men went to the Orient and adopted customs. One in particular concerned the wife of a man. In Korea, the woman keeps her name when married. To get her attention, one says the husband's name and adds "wife." This custom was prevalent in the hood. Mr. Hoskin Thompson had a beautiful wife and home. A white house trimmed with green, roses, hedges—always trimmed—and a tree with fruit that resembled lemons. On a very hot day, I was hoping this was a lemon tree I wanted an ice-cold glass of lemonade. I knocked. "Hello, Mr. Hoskin Thompson Wife, is those lemons?"

"No, sweetheart, it's a (something) derm, but you can make it like lemonade. The difference is the aftertaste. To get rid of this, add lots of sugar. This is a health food."

"Mr. Hoskin Thompson Wife, can I take some?"

"Sure, sweetheart, just don't damage the tree."

"Mr. Hoskin Thompson Wife, do I have to keep bothering you if it's good, and I want more?"

"No, sweetheart, just don't damage it."

"Yes, Ma'am! Thank you, Mr. Hoskin Thompson Wife."

"You are welcome, sweetheart."

After making the lemonade, I lay on the couch, waiting for it to get cold. Also had a glass for Mama when she get off work; then I would head for the library. I dozed off. Mr. Melvin Petty came by to see Mama and woke me up. "Lewis, is this lemonade? You have anymore? Can I have this! Where ya get this?"

He was talking a mile a minute; finally he paused to breathe. I said fast, "Not lemonade! Have plenty of fruit! You can have got from Mr. Hoskin Thompson Wife!"

"Thanks. Lewis, tell ya mama I came by, okay?"

"Okay." Mama was late; they talked the owner of Sunshine Laundry, Mr. Buck Jones, to do half of the hospital garments on Wednesday.

"Cover with plastic, do the end-of-the-week hospital garments on Saturday. Put these sheets on the bottom, the cold sheets on top, cover with plastic, heat rise. What the hospital don't know won't hurt them." They now had to work a half day on Saturday, reduced a six-day to a five-and-half-day work week with the same pay. My mother is beautiful and smart. Rushing to the library, I forgot to tell her that Mr. Melvin Petty came by. The next morning, he came back with two men. He knocked and waited outside; the two men would not be welcome inside.

"Lewis, ya have any more of that lemonade?"

"Yes, sir."

"We will give ya a quarter a jar, what ya say?"

"Yes, sir!"

Next morning, he came back with five additional men and gave me the empty jar. "Lewis, could ya make more?"

"No, sir. I'm using Mama sugar, water, canning jars, and I have to take the money, buy sugar." He did not suggest making up the shortages, and I would not disrespect him by asking for more money. "This is the best I can do."

"Okay, Lewis."

It was the same daily routine except on Sunday. Mama was home and a wrath of questions would need answering. The next Wednesday morning, the men did not come. I thought I had screwed up. I cut back on the sugar, did not make it full strength. Mama came home with the look, yes the look: "Lewis, your ass in trouble." Mama would wait until you were leaving before she confronted you so the thought would be the last on your mine when leaving, and the first on your mind once you returned. Oh man! Where were my aunts and her girlfriends? Anybody to the rescue. "Oh Lord, here goes nothing. Mama, going to the library."

"Lewis, take some of these books back. You are building a library here. You don't have to pay dues?"

"No, Mama, I am the only kid came back three days, help Mr. Simpson White set it up. I think he told his wife I can get away without paying dues. I'm taking some back now." I thought, "Wow! That's what Mama was mad about. I worry about nothing."

"C-ya, Mama."

"Lewis, before ya go, come here."

"Oh hell! That was not it."

"Put the books down. I have somethang to ask ya. Why is those strange men coming to my house?"

I lived up to my reputation. I told my beautiful mother the truth and nothing but the truth.

"I wondered where my sugar was going."

"Mama, take the money out of my drawer, buy more."

"I should. Maybe it will teach ya a lesson. If the men want lemonade, tell them to go to Mrs. Thompson, get the fruit, make their own."

"Mama, you know a man cannot go to Mr. Hoskin Thompson house if he's not home."

"Lewis, the day the men can go to Mr. Thompson house when he's not home, that's the day the men can come to my house when I'm not home. You're listening?"

"No, Mama, I am hearing!" I told (Mr.) Fletcher (Petty) tell his brother (Mr.) Melvin (Petty) what I said.

"Lewis, ya know what the lemonade do?"

"I drank some one time, only one time! You remember the night I told you my ding-dong (penis) hurt? You say go stand by the heater (in summertime, the heater was used to warm water for bathing), than go to bed. This did not help. It would not bend until the next morning!"

Mama was laughing and crying. Look at me start over. I learned at an early age. Performers must know how to milk (when laughter slows down, repeat the punch line). "Mama, it would not bend!"

She was scaring the hell out of me. All she could do motion and point at the door for me to get out, go! The neighborhood watched only entertainment. Watched the world pass you by then tell on you so it slowed down. I was sure the Mothers of Gossip would hear about this and spread the word. I did not make anymore lemonade. I called this a money tree. I am going to the area with the city permission and dig. Maybe a root, stump, or seed to graft and grow the tree. This is not outlandish; I saw on CNN a prehistoric flower bloom. People will not have to buy expensive (hundred dollar) blue pills and put poison drugs in their bodies when they can get the same results naturally. *Believe it or not!*

Calvin E. McLean (Genie Boy/Juice)

Margie Lee H. Bunyon and Beau-Friend

CHAPTER 3

The Day, the Devils Came to Town

My love of anything sweet and not taking care of my teeth took a toll. I had a cavity exposed to the gum and very painful. Mama was saving to get it pulled. This was a problem. It would take an act of Congress. Negroes' access to dentistry in my hometown did not exist. The man she worked for would have to vouch the bill would be paid, but there was a disparity. You paid more because of your race (reasoning, equipment for dental work on Negroes were supposed to be discarded and had to be replaced). The dentist's housekeeper had a house on Steele Street down from us. Her husband was a very dark man who never talked but lived there. She and her daughter resided with the dentist. She was a very beautiful lady from Mississippi. (Today she would be Ms. Soledad O'Brien, television journalist.) They went somewhere and left their beautiful daughter with the dentist. They returned and to this day I have never heard anyone cry like she did. Her little girl just stirred. Mama said, "The white lady was brushing her hair. The dentist told that's his daughter. She hit the baby on the head with the hairbrush. She should have left the little girl with us." (A few years ago, a near community had a killing of a beautiful child named (Ms.) Brittany Locklear. I saw her picture in the newspaper. I had to sit. She was identical, and I'm sure her mother cried the same.) The Ladies of Gossip were talking about the dentist just up and went away. He lost his clients and said he was shooting bad. Rumor said he went to the welfare office and offered to work on poor people for food. He did not take handouts. I witnessed his fate and decided that keeping to myself will maybe prolong my life. One of my many secrets was to sneak to the candy store uptown. I would take the trash out and be rewarded with candy. Her strict rule come in only when nobody was present. (This was not an act of prejudice. Some uptown people still wanted to kill me, and she did not want blood on her hand.) I stood at Johnson Cotton Company (today a pet shop) facing the alley because the five-and-dime was full. The dentist always wore clean clothes, so I was startled on seeing him with tan khaki pants and filthy shirt. He wore a checkered Bear Bryant hat, also dirty. He was accompanied by three men, two tall and a short fat man chewing on a cigar. The men were laughing and telling him to drink this white substance, maybe moonshine (liquor). He obliged like he did not have a choice. When a little was left, he offered it to the others, and the short man told him to keep it and if he needed some more to let him know. The men returned shortly, and the dentist was sprawled out sleeping. One tall man shook him, and there was no response. The short man said, "Move back. I'll wake him up."

He urinated in his face and a man hollered, "Damn, Frank, don't drown him. We not trying to kill him, you know."

Frank said, "We should, but this old piece of shit not worth the price of a rope."

"Well, I gave Millie my word not to hurt him, just make him be gone." One man took his ankles, the other lifted him under his armpits, and Frank carried the hat. I skirted Heinz telephone company's fence. I watched as they threw him in a train cattle car and fastened the latch with a bolt.

Frank said, "It's about time, Cecil, you being after Millie all these years. Now you got her, and that ole boy show back up, you buy the rope."

Beau-friend had many talents. Now I add dentistry. "Lewis, I'm gonna save Cille some money. I will do the dentistry." He tied a string to my tooth and then to the door. He slammed the door. Thank God the string broke. He said, "Lewis, that sucker is deep rooted. It's outa my hands. You gonna need a real dentist I mean one with the right equipment. I will pack with cotton soaked with turpentine. Open your mouth, let the sun shine in. This will keep it dry. Do not eat on this side, no candy or anythang sweet."

Wow! I was the luckiest kid in the world, and I was proud of my big brother, who had many talents. Now I added dentistry. The one I really loved was a hidden talent. He gave me money without me asking. Mama was happy. "Lewis, my prayers have been answered. Dentist are coming to help poor people. We have to go on Price Street tomorrow."

"Thank you, Jesus. I'm gonna get this bad tooth out of my mouth."

Aunt Margaret's house was on the hill with woods and Castle'berry Tobacco Warehouse across the road. We got there, mothers and children. I noticed that some kids had on their Sunday clothes. "Mama, I have to go to Aunt Margaret and do a number two (defecate)." The dental team looked impressive with the white doctor frocks—a short man with black military-style glasses, lady with clipboard flaming red hair (looked like Peggy Bundy in *Married with Children* television program), by which, Mama said she was beautiful. There were two young interns; I gave them the name helpers. Peggy had the mothers sign consent forms. They gave us cornflakes. If you punched the lines, the box became a tray. They gave us little black spoons and poured the milk. The show went on: charts and class on proper care and importance of brushing for our parents' benefit. Our parents were duped, leaving us in the hands of the dentist, Peggy, and the helpers. Our mothers had to work, but Aunt Margaret, a housewife, did not show interest in watching over other people's children. She stayed in her house. They put us in order, small size to large. I was big for my age. Mr. Johnnie Graham was bigger; he would go after me. I admired Johnnie. His father was disabled. As a child, he took on the responsibility. We were playing; he was inside the coal bin plant across the tracks. His father had work there, and I believe the coal dust made him sick. The plant showed gratitude. Theirs was the only family authorized to gather the coal legally. When we did play our favorite game tag, home was the safe base. I was fast; he would get almost home, speed up, tag, let him catch me. I noticed why he tried hard to win; his mother would be peeping out the door, laughing at us. Of course, I let him win after she called him to do his chores before it got dark. He had a beautiful sister, Delois.

The trailer was positioned on a trail. Exiting the trailer the ladies would place hands on your shoulders and guild you towards the path towards W. B. Wicker High School. Dealing with children this act prevented going to the front and tell your ordeal to other children. The group got smaller. There was a small room with a small piano; we sang. A helper played; the other one was a conductor. She moved her hands. "Sing louder, children, sing louder!" We did with all our hearts: "Row Row Row Ya Boat," "Jimmy Crack Corn," "Old Mac Donald," "Do Ya Ears Hang Low." We obliged. Only two of us were left. I was next. Johnnie was bigger. I was seated in the dentist's chair. A rare event—the complete team were with me; Johnnie was left alone. The dentist put the clamp on the bad tooth, left knee in my chest, and pulled. I screamed. He pulled. I screamed. I looked at him for sympathy. I remember the only time he talked. Peggy had a pleading look on her face, and he said, "He's going to lose the tooth in time. This is a premature."

She told him, "You won't do it? Do it for me! I will keep the tooth!" He was looking at Peggy. I looked to my left. Maybe the helpers would stop this madness. They were smiling, looking at Peggy also. The dentist was orchestrating Peggy's actions. The clipboard was in front; she was rubbing her private part as I screamed. Pull, pull, pull! I screamed, screamed, screamed; Peggy rubbed, rubbed, rubbed. The tooth was yanked out. I screamed; but, Peggy screamed louder, dropped the clipboard, threw her head back, and her hair came off. I pissed in my pants, thankful I had used the bathroom at Aunt Margaret's. If not, I would have shit also. Mama said, "She has beautiful hair." Yes, not hers. With her eyes closed, her right hand was on the wall. She appeared weak and about to fall down. The helpers burst out laughing. The dentist did not respond. He acted like this was normal and his job. The helpers cleaned the blood off me, never looking in my eyes, just smiling. Peggy gained her composure, picked up the clipboard and horsehair. She squatted down, hugged me at the door, and gave me a bag of fruit. I went down the steps, looked to my left—a trash can surrounded with rotten fruit. I looked in the bag—rotten fruit. I followed suit. At the end of the trail, I waited for Johnnie. He was walking slowly, teary-eyed. He looked like he was in shock. He wanted to say something but did not know how or why. I looked back in disbelief. The ladies were picking up the rotten fruit and bagging them for the afternoon sessions. We walked in silence. We got to the split Bland Drugstore, did not play tag or make eye contact. We just went home. I do not know how many kids were molested or abused. I did not tell Mama. Mama let me off the hook by saying, "Lewis, sometimes not knowing is better." I spared her the agony of knowing and not able to do anything about it. I let myself off the hook thinking that nobody would believe a kid's word over white people's who took time to help poor people. I blamed myself. If I did not have the bad tooth, this would not have happened. Some children had what I was lacking, courage, and told their mothers.

Next year, Mama was standing at the front door, prior to leaving for work. "Lewis, the dentist is on Price Street today. Y'all go get ya teeth check and clean. Ya hear me, Lewis?"

"Yes, Mama." Mama's custom is tell you something in advance, then keep reminding you. I noticed this was not her. She looked back with an inkling that I might as well be talking to the walls. The children were not going, and I would not tell her why.

I never lied to my mother. (Mr. Bill Clinton (President) would be proud knowing my concept at an early age "don't ask, don't tell.")

"Lewis, we are going to the dentist?"

"Naw, Genie Boy, we are going to the park!"

"Okay, Lewis, I'm ready to go." Washington Park was supposed to be named for its location (off Washington Avenue), the street named after George Washington. In reality, the Negro park was name after the slave owner. Many years later, the name was changed to Horton Park after Mr. W. T. Horton, a black man. (Amazingly, actions by one of my heroes, a white policeman, laid the groundwork for the black park. Officer Poe will be introduced in the story in Chapter Four, "You are The Man, until The Man Come!") The park had children everywhere, and I noticed some had on their Sunday clothes. No one suggested going to the park; it just seemed a natural thing kids would do. Bind together after exposure to the devil and his harem. Beau-friend, Crybaby, and other young men were sitting on a picnic table. I sneaked down to hear and pick up new cuss words. One thing they knew how to do well, cuss. This time they were serious, no fooling around. Crybaby said, "We oughta go get them for what they did to our brothers and sisters."

Beau-friend said, "We oughta go rock 'em!"

"Yeah let's go!" We moved out.

"Genie Boy, go back. You are too little."

Beau-friend looked at me and smiled. Wow! He did not tell me go back watch my little brother Genie boy. I was floating, could not feel my legs with my hero, mentor, my big brother, Beau-friend. People got on top of the warehouse with big rocks to rain down on them. The signal: "When I lower my hat, everybody throws to all the ammo's gone." Beau-friend gave the signal. Boom! Boom!

Rocks hitting the trailer. The door swung open, and the little white man bolted out. White frock literally in the wind. He jumped in the car and veered out of the woods fast. Beau-friend said, "I don't think we have to worry about them next year. Everybody keep this to themselves, hear me, Lewis?"

"Yeah, Beau-friend."

We came out of the woods at the park. Children on the opposite bank were cheering. Genie Boy and the kids turned back told the other kids our plan. We were heroes. I never told anyone my ordeal except you, the reader. I was holding my two rocks to throw and hit the devil. I hit trees. The little white man was moving too fast. The kids treated me special. There was a long line for the big slide. "Lewis, come up front." They would let me go until I got tired. Mama never asked about the dentist. The hood have ears and noses. You cannot fart without somebody hearing or smelling it. Mama knew I looked up to Beau-friend. To keep me from choosing between them, she never asked. She sold herself short a 100 percent record—I never lied to her, but would have to stretch the truth. If she asked, "Did you go to the dentist like I say?"

"Yes, Mama. He was not in. Left rushing like his life depended on it." I thanked her for not making me decide. Beau-friend would have lost. Mama carried me for nine months just to have me on the hottest day in a decade. Mothers are Love and Genius.

Fast forward: It's ironic; the best commander in the army is a white man, the worst, a black man. These stories will prevail in future writings. The best was Colonel Jerald Thompson, killed in Iraq by our air force enforcing the no-fly zone. Stationed at Fort Bragg, North Carolina, he ordered me to attend a class at the Welcome Center. "Make him a block of instruction for returning soldiers (three soldiers killed wives after coming home)." It was a two-week course. On entering the classroom, no one told me it was a wife transition class or perceived to be. There were seventeen women with an instructor and an assistant. It dawned on me, "I'm still performing. Life is an act. You are always on stage." All eyes were on me. I dropped everything and shouted, "I have died and gone to heaven! Pause, or Hell!" The ladies burst out laughing. This broke the ice. "I hope another man come. I have been in many situations where I'm the only man, it's call church!" Wow! I liked the atmosphere; the ladies laughed at my funnies. "Ladies, this is serious. Please do not ask me for a man point of view. I can only give you mine. Do not go home. Sargent McLean says, 'I do not want to be on a hit list to get my butt kick at least seventeen times.'"

On Thursday, the second week, there was a sensitivity class. The instructor was beautiful. She said, "People say I'm beautiful and should fix my teeth." She put her hand to the mouth when talking or laughing. Well, I go to counseling for this. When I was little, we were poor. People came and pulled teeth without pain medicine. This white lady was telling complete strangers, and I was a grown ass man who never told anyone. This was not the time or place. "Sargent McLean, it's your turn."

"I will pass. It's someone I have to tell first."

"Make sure you do, Sargent McLean. It will be a new day in your life. Ladies were telling heart-wrenching things—rape by stepfathers, pastors, neighbors, and the most outlandish story. I knew her husband in Germany and made up my mind to find a way to confront this bozo (clown). I am omitting the graphic details. He tied her up and made her watch as he had sex with his stepdaughter. The class was supposed to be confidential; however, he was arrested as he got off the airplane. People say the little girl dramatized the act, doing show and tell. Teachers, principal, counselor, got involved. The highlight got people to bring up things that were buried. Attempt to move forward even if you need counseling.

At home, I took a trash bag in the bathroom. Put all dental supplies, excluding toothbrushes and toothpaste, in the bag. *"Yo'bo* (Korean for sweetheart), what are you doing?"

"Fixing to make dinner, wae (way) oh (means why)?"

"An-Jew (sit), I have something to tell you. You always say why I make you guys go to the dentist and I do not." I told my story. She was teary-eyed and said, "Dad that was nothing but devils set on destroying children lives." I only told this story to my wife and you.

As I am physical and mentally abuse I noticed five degrees from a prominent university on the wall. One day I will go check the archives find the devil and his harem. (Photos will be posted, robertmclean350@gmail.com.)

Note:

1) God, forgive them; they know not what they do.
2) Give me a woman, black dentist, or both, please.
3) Found beautiful black woman dentist. She moved back north to care for her mother.
4) Found a black dentist, "Hometown Dental Office" Raeford, North Carolina, the greatest since sliced bread.
5) Sitting in the dentist's chair, I asked Ms. Angie (my daughter's nickname), "Where is my dentist?" "He moved on." I started shaking. It may seem like nothing to her but meant the world to me. She patted me on the right side of my chest about ten seconds. I made up my mind, the buck stops here! I'm going to be all right!

I am closing this chapter with a beautiful song lyrics I heard in Frazier Bottoms, West Virginia.

"If it was not for the Lighthouse where would this Ship be."

Answer: (Ship) Wrecked

A very rich man running for the highest office in the land said, "I'm not concern about the poor, very poor. We have a safety net in place for them." Some safety nets are flawed and need to be mended. Three beautiful ladies who contributed to my plight positively:

1) My mother, Mrs. Lucille (Cille) McLean said, "Lewis, fear only fear itself. Now what are you scared of."
2) Fort Bragg Welcome Center Instructor said, "Sargent McLean, confront your fears even if you need counseling."
3) My dental assistant, Ms. Michelle, said, "Mr. McLean, writing is therapy and reading also. I will love (keyword) to read an excerpt until the books are published."

Rarely you get what you ask for unless it's trouble (*Smile*).

(Me)

John T. Hollingsworth (Woodchuck)

CHAPTER 4

"You Are the Man, Until the Man Comes."

"Reb" was a man of God who strove for the betterment of mankind. A short form of "rebellion," not for the conservative (Johnnie Rebel). For reverends who have R-E-S-P-E-C-T (thank you Queen of Soul, Ms. Aretha Franklin) from the church and community, to be called "Reb" was a honor. (A present-day "Reb," The Honorable Reverend Al Sharpton. Amazingly, a black man in charge of RNC (formerly) as a guest on his show *Politic Nation* on MSNBC always bid farewell by saying, "Thank you, Reb." We call this man Bar Be Q Steele. With the power of the Republicans, he rendered an apology to a racist bigot who called himself a journalist. Mama says, "Lewis, God don't like ugly." The racist bigot journalist talked on his radio show for three days, nine hours, about a law student's life. I will call her "Ms. One and Done." Her only case was "Sue the racist bigot journalist for slander." I do not know law.

A new reverend and family came to town. His name was Reverend J. R. Hampton. We called him "Reb." The community embraced the Hampton family, except the big ballers. The basketball goal in Fleming Cafe and Groceries was at the back door of Blandonia Presbyterian Church and the Hampton quarters. The big ballers were inventive when it came to cursing. Showmanship with game and mouth. The better you are the more shit you talk. (Today it's called trash talking.) Reb Hampton came to the big ballers and said,

"Stop the cursing! Stop or the goal will come down." After he left, the brave souls spoke up.

"Who he think he is? The white man says we can put the goal on his land. The goal was here before he came. It will be here when he leaves."

"Yeah, man, sho ya right!"

I liked Reb Hampton; he did not send word like Reverend McMillan. This preacher (he did not get the title Reb, reason unknown) before him he deliver the message.

"Who he think he is? Come out here telling us what to do? Yeah, Fuck 'em!" I counted five paces not Catholic and made five cross your heart, waiting for the lightning bolt. The cursing slowed down, not completely stopped. There were good days and bad. One big baller went against the grain. He played ball quietly and let his game do the talking. He did not miss often, especially getting to his sweet spot, the right corner. His name was Mr. Larry Taylor. If the big ballers were like him, they would not be in a losing situation with God and Reb Hampton. I liked watching and cheering for Beau-friend. He has a game and a filthy mouth. We had to wait for the big ballers to leave in order to play. A new teacher came up. He was big with muscles everywhere, including his ears. His name was Mr. John Marshall.

"Children, come over here! I bring a bus on Saturdays. Will your parents let you go? I have outside and inside basketball courts. Finish playing you can take showers and get a hot meal before I bring you back."

The official leader spoke up. "Sir, we need to bring a note!"

"No, I will take your word. I will meet you here at nine next Saturday morning." I liked Mr. Marshall right away. He was going to take our words, no questions asked. Well, what Mrs. Lucille McLean didn't know couldn't hurt her. Mr. Marshall was true to his words. He took us to a school called A&T University. He got paid for the number of children signed in. The local kids had these resources and didn't take advantage. They saw kids playing, having fun in their neighborhood. They came out in droves. Mr. Marshall's plan worked to perfection. Talking about Superman (code name) Mr. John Marshall we were excited and talking too loud. The Ladies of Gossip were on the porch. Mama, looking at me, said, "Y'all ever wonder where the children goes on Saturdays? It seems they get missing."

Aunt Dot had the only television. "I wonder, the house usually full on Saturday morning, watching cartoons and laughing. I ask John Thomas did he do somethang. He say, him and Lewis had a mud fight. Agnes made them stop and hug, so he donna know why they not coming."

I was not going to be close-minded and say Mama did not know the answer already. I said, "Please God, do not let Mama put me on the spot in front of everybody. My reputation of not lying to her do not have to be proven." She did not ask. Hey y'all, that was a close call. Mr. Marshall have a lot of kids coming we should fess(confess) up. I think Beau-friend told Mama. They were jealous we had Superman and all they had was themselves.

All good things must come to an end and bad things linger on. A light-skinned curly-haired boy came to my team, turned, and pointed to a black midget. "That man over there say, y'all come back here, people are gonna to kill ya." We got offended, not at the situation but because this bougie nigger was talking as if we did not understand proper English. Midget man did not win a game all summer. Man playing with children, skill, not age should prevail. We had a winning plan derived during pitching horseshoes by Mr. Benny Lee Smith. "The stronger team plays the opponent, take no prisoners! Our segregated team will make you and others strive to integrate. Losing will be your way of life."

"Mr. Marshall, the little man sent that boy over to give us a message." He hurried and confronted midget man, who was ball less. Blame the messenger. Don't shoot the messenger! Mr. Marshall, thank you. This was the best summer of our lives. What the little man said didn't bother us; we had a greater fear. We did not tell our mothers our secret. Mr. Marshall laughed and said, "I figure it out. When you do tell your mothers, say 'thank you' for me."

Word spread like wildfire—Old man Fleming will not support the big ballers. He has to battle with God, Reb Hampton, and church members/ customers. I liked Reb Hampton immediately. He went face-to-face, not like Reverend McMillan (did not get the title Reb for some ungodly reason), sent a messenger; lucky he was not shot! He did not rush to judgment. They got chances for redemption. The big ballers were offended; somebody was telling them what they could not do and the tag alone had a real Superman. We were supposed to grow up like them. Beau Friend attacked the character of Mr. Marshall. "Y'all think muscle head came to take ya away to play. Wrong, he has a girlfriend he comes to see. He used y'all." Out of the clear blue, as I was standing on church ground behind the goal, these words, too cherished, just flowed.

"Beau-friend, I don't care if he has ten girlfriends. 'Mr. Marshall Is The Man, until The Man Comes.'"

"Lewis, you keep trying to be smart. I'm gonna dust you off." Mr. Marshall did use us, and his plan worked to perfection. The have kids saw the have-not kids having the time of their lives in their neighborhood.

In the redemption period, cursing slowed. A word uttered, the game stopped with all eyes on the back door of the Hampton quarters, hoping he did not hear it—not realizing, we have to worry about the one who hears everything in heaven. I had a solution. I did not share the fear of being called names and being belittled by the big ballers. Embrace God and Reb Hampton like the tag alone did with God and Mr. Marshall (the first black Superman, sorry Mr. O'Neil II and Mr. Howard III) (great basketball players and humanitarians). Invite him seventy-five feet play and pray. If they ever invite him to play I suggest he wear the collar, cross, or both. The big ballers are devil made.

One day, a man walked toward us, talking education, smack, or jive (trash talking without cursing). "I got game! I am the beat of the drum! I am the best! Nobody can stop me! I know nobody out here can stick me! I am gonna show ya what I got, but I'm gonna take it light on you chumps." He was true to every word. Best player I had ever seen. Most of the big ballers had a single strong point. He displayed all talents and like he said, "I got game!" God had answered my prayers. "This is the man I will imitate, watch, study, and make a mental picture of every move. I will be a replica of Mr. Herbert Siler." I added my flavor. He went to his toes, set shot. I jumped jump shot. I tried his way. I did not have the strength for long range. Jumping allowed. I practiced, morning, evening, and supper time. I would pick the time to showcase my new talents. One of the greatest moments of my life was when Mr. Herbert Siler confronted me after I became a top-notch (word provided by the Brits) player. "You know, you stole my shot!"

"Yes, sir." We laughed. Once he read my memoir or told by his sons (Mr.) Raymond, (Mr.) Jake Louis, (Mr.) Derrick, I also stole his attitude. "I got game! Nobody can stop me! I am the beat of the drum!"

A blessing or hindrance—big ballers who could not control their weakness stopped coming.

The enforcer was a man nobody messed with, Mr. Dave Smith. Rumor had it he was meaner than a junkyard dog. He had reasons, it was his making. He spent time in New York City and wanted to bring the atmosphere down south completely. (Watch the movie *White Men Can't Jump*.) Will give a visual. Before Mr. Herbert Siler, Beau-friend would always choose me. Game on the line, I usually missed the shot or passed. I was called names and pushed (fight). After Mr. Herbert Siler, I picked the time to perform—Friday when the court was packed and pay day. I passed waiting for my moment. "Lewis, throw to me." I would drive and dish to Larry in the corner. Wrong answer, my Beautiful Friend (feel the cockiness). Everybody knew we gonna run our bread and butter play. Larry passed to me. He looked surprised. All the torment he delivered on me was a phase; it did not hold water. "Okay, Lewis, take the shot!" I swished from the top of the key. Larry said, "Good shot, Lewis."

Beau-friend acted like this was nothing. No big deal. He went to Mr. Dave Smith and said, "Double or nothing." That's it; he got mad money on the line.

Mr. Dave Smith said, "Oh hell! No! I know a scam when I see one. You done taught ya little brother how to ball when we were not looking!"

Beau-friend turned with a challenge. "Where ista next chumps!" We had a winning combination. He for money, and I for the love of the game. I vowed get back money lost. As the ball went in the hoop, I started saying money! People started saying, "Lewis shot is like money in ther (not misspelled) bank."

I did something the big ballers with too much pride failed to do or would not do. "Reb Hampton! Like to shoot hoops?" He did not have game, but had the big three on his side, Father, Son, Holy Spirit. Knowing this, I came to the conclusion he did not have to cover with the collar or cross; we were the only ones playing. At high school ball, he never missed a game. Always sat in the holy spot and we made eye contact, smiled. Oh God! I love you, and the inspirational Reverend (Reb) Mr. James R. Hampton. A song asked,

"Why The Good Die Young?" I will give my answer. "You want the good home with you." Thank you, God the Father, I spent too short a time with this great man whom I loved.

"Lewis, the things I do is for you hustling." One thing I did not approve of was chasing women on my behave. I could learn to experience this myself. I had something he did not, time. Time is money, then, now, and later. I had a fine-tuned game, and I practiced; however, my big brother was the better player. Friction started when people made comments. "Lewis is the best player." The devil is always working. Brother love became stranded. A passage in the holy book says the older brother will serve the younger. I did not take his birthright. A blessing, I did not have to ask for money or hustle. My big brother took care of me. Beau Friend would put his hand in my pocket and grasp money. How much? If I am wrong he took his money. He would say,

"Lewis, ya don't know the money in ya pocket, niggers will steal it." He let the devil come between us. "Lewis, one on one, let's go!"

"Beau-friend, you did not bet on yourself, did ya?" The game to me pitted brother against brother, nothing to prove, but he had a different outlook. Win at all cost. He would not pass the throne. After losing to get off the hook he could say, "Lewis learned well. I taught him everything he knows. Yet I'm going to teach him a lesson don't fuck with me." Strong start, weak ending. Night life not practicing paid a toll. I let up. He made a hard foul; there was no justification, no need. I got up and walked away. He hit me in the back with the ball and screamed, "Com' on, Lewis, show me ya can take it! Prove ya can take it!" Reb Hampton was looking out of his back window. I think this was the straw that broke the camel's back. Next day, like the city of Jericho, the basketball goal came tumbling down. (Ironic, he gave them fourteen days.)

Across the tracks from Bland Drugstore was a big white house. Mr. Sam Johnson's family resided there. There was a goal in the front yard; big ballers came with the venom (cursing). Mr. Sam Johnson made his sons take it down. We were bored to death and got mad. Mr. Marshall said, "We left too soon, pretty girls came to see the boys from out of town." The cafeteria ladies spread the word throughout the neighborhood. The boys were so nice and good-looking. The beautiful ladies were right on! (Thank you, Civil Rights Movement for this slogan.) I asked Ms. Carolyn, and Ms. Judy, "Would you ask your father could we nail a bicycle rim to the tree?"

"No cursing."

"Yes," we said in unison. "Thank you, Mr. Sam Johnson."

"You are welcome, children! No cussing!"

"Yes, sir!"

We had a big problem; the ball was egg-shaped. If we bounced it, it had a mind of its own. We laughed and made rules to adjust to this shortcoming. Bounce with two hands or take two steps. I compared our feelings to the mule kept locked down. Release him and he will run and kick up his heels. Nothing was taken seriously; it was all fun. A white policeman drove up, parked along the side of Railroad Street and watched us play. Rule of thumb—never make eye contact with the police. I glanced and noticed he laughed when someone made a basket with the wobble ball. He got out and said, "Y'all come here."

One kid held back. "Y'all go ahead. I'm gonna ask can I use the toilet." The policeman was named Officer Poe.

"Y'all having a whale of time, I see. This the only place you have to play?"

"Yes, sir!" I gave instant respect. We have a mutual friendship. I recognized him immediately as the policeman who saved my sanity.

He said, "Naw, I don't see him." He gave me a new look on life. When beaten by the police, Negroes were hit in the head. Name of this act was called "nigger knocking." Result: afterward you stare at the wall, piss, and shit on yourself. "Sir, the goal behind Blandonia Presbyterian Church was taken down. A teacher Mr. John Marshall took us to A&T University. The locals didn't like outsiders, so this is it."

"No, son, this is not it. I know a place with a new surface, and we put up new chain nets. It's across the other tracks at the school. Why you don't go there?" All eyes were on me. I did not recall this was a one-on-one conversation.

"Sir, we were told never go across those tracks. We do we will be arrested and go to jail. Never go on that school playground, we're not allowed."

"Well, I'm the police. Someone says you cannot go across the tracks and play at the school, tell them to see me. Two things you cannot do, curse or fight. Make myself clear?"

"Yes, sir!"

By the way opening the car trunk, he took out a brand-new basketball. "I think the ball you have won't make it." We laughed. He tossed me the ball; I was now sure he remembered our encounter. He said, "This is a keepsake."

"Thank you, sir!"

"Well, what are you waiting for? You gonna play basketball or you wanna go to jail!"

"Basketball, sir!" We went across the Berlin Wall—the railroad tracks that divided the people. Mr. Sam Johnson, who gave us the green light to play and made this happen, a special thank you.

Bestowed on his wife and children, Tick, Carolyn, Chamberlain, Jesse, Judy, and Spider, God bless you.

We had to get on the kid that was scared of the policeman. He needed a convincing story or he would be branded for life, teased forever. After hearing his story, we decided not to tease him; you could find yourself on the witness stand. He told the story one time. We all shouted, "We did not hear you!" The meat of his story minus the bullshit: A white man was hit by a car on Horner Blvd. He left the Laundromat to check on the man who was knocked out. The car did not stop, and people saw him check his wallet for identification. I thought his name maybe Washington, Grant, or Lincoln. I shouted, "Hold it! Spare me the agony. Mrs. Lucille McLean son did not hear a damn thang!" Kids started saying, "Hear what! What ya say! Cannot hear ya! Speak up, man!" We were off the hook. Grown-ups said that we young niggers had a hard head, deaf and dumb. Now was a good time to prove them right. Sho, ya right, Clang!

Across the street was a sky blue house with a swing on the poach. An old lady would watch us play. We had a court, ball, and permission to play. The big ballers dared not come here. It was out of their comfort zone. The old lady did not have a problem until children started coming. The segregation plan went into effect. The stronger team played the opponent; then we juked and jived among ourselves. The old lady screamed, "Niggahs! Go back cross them there tracks! Shame on ya white kids playing with niggahs. Do ya parents know ya playing with niggahs? Niggahs! You betterah run, niggahs the police coming."

The tall kid said, "Go in the house! They not bothering you!" Wow! She listened and went in the house. A very short kid said, "Are ya gonna run?"

"Why?"

"She gonna call the police."

"Well, let her. We are not crazy enough to come over here without permission. The police says we are allow to play here." They did all right! Staley (Mr. Jackie McLean) says, "Officer Po-Poe."

"Hey, Staley, let's not disrespect him. We could still be shooting in the bicycle rim with egghead." "Yeah, Clang, you are right."

"Naw, man, we are both right."

The Mr. Marshall, Officer Poe plan or concept worked. They had not been using facilities taken for granted by the have-mores (description of affluent people used by MSNBC's Mr. Ed Shultz, and President George W. Bush), and having the time of their lives. Like the bougies at A&T University, children came out in droves. Reasoning: "School is in. We came to teach with a chip on our shoulders. You not one of us. We show no mercy, take no prisoners." My vivid imagination was running wild as I pictured the old lady steaming in her house at what had taken place. The goals were the same distance. Reb Hampton's doorway to the basketball goal and the old lady's doorway is seventy-five feet. I stand for, I stand, I cannot stand no more! She came out of the house like a fly in hell, screaming loudly, "Niggahs, leave this place! You teaching these white children to lie and steal! Begone, you niggahs! I'm calling the police 'cause you niggers are teaching these white children too cuss and sin. You niggahs are sinners! You betterah run, niggahs, you betterah run!"

The ball went out of bounds, and I saw a police car on the next street. Before, she ranted on the front porch. Now seeing the police car, she went in the yard and pointed him out for us. "Niggers, that there is the police, y'all betterah run."

The police see her pointing and drives up. This is God's work; we were supposed to be here. It is Officer Poe. "Y'all been cussing?"

"No, sir!"

"Y'all been fighting?"

"No, sir!"

The tall kid said, "That lady have been calling them out of their names."

"I will deal with her in a minute. Any problems I need to be made aware of?"

The tall kid said, "Yes, sir! We do have a problem."

"What is it, son?"

"They won't break up their teams. I'm tired of losing. We have not won a game since they started coming. The game is twenty one." Your team get eleven points before the other team score they lose. This is refer as being skunk. We get to nine points we would say S-T-W-B which means skunk the white boys. Most have never score a basket it would be etched in stone family name in shame the wrath of hell if a white boy score on you. This is serious business. Officer Poe turned away, laughing. Turned back red-faced.

"You telling me you want to play on the same team, but they refused."

"Yes, sir!"

He could not get a hold of himself; he laughed, laughed as a relief. Maybe he thought the shoe would be on the other foot. He gained his composure and said, "I'm sure you going to work something out." Laughing aside, he turned to the old lady and shouted, "You leave these children alone! Call the station or bother these children again, I'm taking you to jail! Now get in the house! Don't come out again bothering these children!" No cussing no fighting! Black and white

114

kids were equal in the eyes of this great policeman, Officer Poe. We shouted, "Yes, sir!"

The kids hashed a plan. I strongly believe Officer Poe had given inputs. He should have said, "I'm sure we are going to work something out." I have the ball so nobody had to wait to play. I would go early. The white kids would come in the afternoon. By then the deck would be stacked; all they could do was lose. This morning I counted fifteen kids who had the first fifteen games. A tall kid and a shorter kid shot for first pick and the ball. The tall kid won and pointed to me. "What's your name?"

"Lewis."

"My name Chris. I got Lewis." Then he picked the smallest kid named Monte. We were a winning combination: Monte, long range, Chris on the boards, and Mr. Multi-talent (me). The black kids started dragging in.

"Lewis, you gonna stop, so we can keep our team."

"Nope, these guys have the first fifteen games, and I'm not waiting three or four hours to play. I'm having fun kicking butts. Y'all can pout or play, it's up to you." They followed suit. We literally were having fun. No white cloud (an outlet) hanging over our heads. Now you lose, blame it on the white team mates. We were forced to integrate or we didn't play. (Thank you, Officer Poe. Children could not envision this ever happening.)

Chris's mom drove a white convertible, Bonneville, dressed to the nines—all white and glitter of diamonds. Before, Chris would throw shoes and towels in the car and then slam the door. We laughed at his hi-jinks and came to the conclusion he was a sore loser. Today he ran to his mother excitedly. "Mom, we haven't lost a game all day! I'm not ready to go. Can I stay, Mom?"

She did the unthinkable; she spoke. This was the first time in our lives a white lady did this. None of the Negroes responded. "Lewis, my mom says hello."

I sheepishly waved and said, "Hello." She left and we picked up where we left off kicking butts. Chris's mom returned with refreshment. We stood back as the items were taken out of the car. "I have to go back. I did not bring enough glasses."

"Mom, this more than enough." There was a mixture of juices, pineapple being the main course of drink. He poured for me. I drank and looked to pass to a black. Chris took my glass. I poured, he drank. Chris takes the picture and pour. We picked up glasses, no matter who drank from it. We thanked her and said, "It's delicious."

"Mom, this have been the best day of my life. I made up for all the games I lost."

"This mean you are not going to throw your shoes in the car?" (In the presence of this beautiful lady proper English prevailed.)

"Not today, Lewis. Mom, I'm sorry."

We went "Ahhhh, how sweeteee." Chris's mom blushed. We laughed. The first time ever in the presence of a white lady and top it off, first time making a white lady's cheeks red. It appeared she was staring at you. I would say this situation was a first for her too. Many black men were in Caldonia Prison for looking at white women. They even had a name for this crime called "reckless eye balling." When attrition occurred, white men with chains and beautiful white women made up shortages by going to towns. A lady would walk by, drop something, and bend. All Negroes caught looking would be charged with the crime and chained, taken to prison for a year. (Police acted as judge and jury.) (Today, there is same mentality; seventeen-year-old (Mr.) Trayvon Martin of Sanford Florida was walking home, armed with a can of iced tea and a bag of skittle candy for his brother; he was gunned down by George (9 mm) Zimmerman. This man and police acted as judge, jury, and executioner. Oh God, these are some problematic times, then, now, and later.)

"Mom, can Lewis come to the house sometimes?"

"Sure, if he want to."

"Thanks for the invite, but my fun days are about over. I have to work to buy my school clothes."

"You have to work in order to buy school clothes?"

"Man, I am not rich like somebody I know." We laughed.

"Mom, can I work?"

"We will talk about it later, Chris."

"Lewis, this is the best day of my life. Thanks and good-bye."

"You are welcome. However, we only say good-bye to the dead. This is the beginning, not the end. So, we says c-ya man."

"Okay, Lewis, c-ya man."

"Y'ell man, c-ya."

People in a blue pickup truck started packing and putting the old lady's household goods on the truck. She had a handkerchief to wipe tears. It appeared she wanted to say something and did not know how or why. She did not owe us anything, not even an explanation. Monte said, "Let's tell her good-bye and good riddance." I'm sure it was hard for her to comprehend and swallow, children are innocent. Hate is a learned behavior that she knew well. The scene was too devastating for her: black and white kids playing together, a beautiful red-faced (blushing) white lady dressed to the nines in all white diamonds galore serving punch, and they were drinking out of the same glasses. She was too naive to realize that this way of life, this ideology whose foundations were based on racism, bigotry, and hate would be destroyed by open-minded children. (Today, conservative radio hosts understand these principles and a green light, destroy women and children.) "No, Monte! Let her leave in peace."

The school yard was overflowing with children. We integrated to a degree the kick-butt team now played together and lived up to the standard—take no prisoners. It appeared the black kids had a defeatist attitude until Officer Poe arrived. Hit a shot; he punched the air, yeah! The black kids would play harder in order to get this recognition. Hit a shot and waited for the response. He motioned, "Come here. A lot of children here today, huh?"

"Yes, sir!"

"I notice some kids only play one game, some kids stay on the court."

"Yes, sir!"

"Well, I have an idea, so the less talent children can have fun. We fix the courts at the school on Horner Blvd. You know where it is?"

"Yes, sir."

The only difference was we did not put up chain nets. "The houses too close, and the way y'all swish them, the people may take out a warrant for disturbing the peace." He laughed. God I know I loved this man; he even had a sense of humor.

"You know my rule to live by?"

"Yes, sir. No cussing, no fighting."

"Okay, son. See y'all over there next Saturday. Any problems I need to know about?"

"No, sir! Thank you, sir!"

"Hey, y'all. Officer Poe want the pros to go to a new location, so kids not as good can play more. I think he is behind the scene, and his plan to make us break up and play with the white guys (status upgraded). I think these guys told they have a problem. We bogart (take charge) the courts. He want us to go next Saturday to the school playground on Horner Blvd."

"Hey, Clang! We have to go uptown in the white neighbor?"

"Yeah, man. Officer Poe says go, no if, an', or but. He tell ya to jump off the Empire State Building would ya?"

"Yeah, Clang, what about you?"

"Negroes, are ya crazy! You know how high that building is?"

"Yeah, Clang, would ya jump!"

"Are ya crazy! Sure I'm gonna jump and display my home training bow, extend my arm, and say, 'Y'all first.' The wagon train leave Bland's Drugstore at ten next Saturday. You are late, come play here. Do not walk thru the white neighborhood alone. Let's not forget the last Negro man almost caught in the white lady was tar and feather. It took gallons of moonshine and gasoline to get the stuff off him."

"Clang, you mix the shine and gas together."

"Naw, man, you drink the shine to dull the pain 'cause they douse the gas on ya ass and scrap ya with steel-teeth brushes. The people have only one concern. They do not want to be an accident and would ask ya, 'Do ya smoke?'" After all he went through, he caught in the white lady this time. Loud screams sounded like a call for help. White men burst in; he jumped back off the bed, standing on the floor and still had a foot of dick in her. Maybe true white men witnessed this and spread the word. They hanged his ass. Drug him up and down main street as white people cheered and applauded. Black men called him horse or mule, said, "Hey horse." Reply yell, but I got a mule dick and vice versa. Folklore in the hood, he never kissed a lady while having sex. He did not like tasting his dick. A gypsy fortune teller's son was a star in Western movies, name Lash La'rue. A fortune teller she was asked why she did not see the men coming and save the Negro man, she replied, "I only deal with white souls." After hearing this, she lost Negro clients who had to enter her house through the back door. Out of respect for the man and family I will not reveal his name. In admiration, I called him "Mr. Three Legs."

"Lewis, I heard Office Poe call ya 'son' again."

"Naw, man, you was listening, not hearing. Hearing, you could play back what I said, 'Yes, sir dad.'"

"Let's not go down the yellow brick road. We are bless 'cause we are fatherless children. God always put men in our life to keep us on the narrow path."

"Damn, Clang, where ya get this stuff? I do not listening to my mother. I hear her and just play it back! So clean out your ears and hear your mothers. You will be surprise how beautiful and smart they are."

"Yeah, Clang, c-ya."

"Not if I see ya first, okay, y'all, c-ya."

An amazing feat—everyone was early. God do great work in mysterious ways. My friends were not lazy and good-for-nothing; they were lazy and good-for-something. "I will call you my friends if everyone on time. Not I have another name to call y'all. I'm going to tell you a bedtime story, and no I'm not going tuck ya in, just ponder when ya go to sleep. This may motivate ya be on time. Indians have this cowboy tied up, straw and wood at his feet."

"White cowboy, Clang?"

"Negro, have ya ever seen a black cowboy in the movies?"

"No! I did not want to be so mean! Mama said, 'The only dumb question is the one not ask.'"

"I did not mean to shoot ya down. The cowboy is a dark skin white man. He's Italian and named Lash La'rue." We laughed. "'Chief, before ya light me up, could I tell my horse something?' 'Yell, paleface.' Whisper, the horse took off, returned with a naked blonde lady. The Indians snatch her off. 'Chief, could I tell my horse something again?' Whisper, the horse took off, returned with a naked redhead lady. The Indians snatch her off. 'Chief, please allow me another.' 'Yell, paleface.' Whisper, horse took off returned with a naked black hair lady. The Indians snatch her off. 'Sorry for delaying the bar-be-q, Chief. The last request, will ya release my right arm?' He motion for the horse to come close. With all his might, he hit the horse between the eyes. The horse drop to his knees and Lash La'rue shouted, 'I said "posse" ya fool! "Posse!"'"

My friends were dumb-witted. Slowly, one by one, "I got it, Clang!" To keep from being called Lewis and his pussies, I mean posse, they beat the ten o'clock deadline.

Adults were on the porch, and if looks could kill, we would have been slaughtered. On the right side, There was about two hundred feet woods with two white cars. The leader had to be brave only after seeing the police cars. "Y'all quit huddling around me and space out. Clang, we need space to fight."

"Negro, please. I need space to run. I do not want to be tripping over ya." We broke the tension with light laughter. The woods where Officer Poe was parked now houses my bank, BB&T. Thank you, Jesus, you never disappoint—a quite prayer murmured from the supposedly brave leader. There was a loud commotion, a short man was trying to hold back a tall kid with a blue shirt on. The buttons were ripped off; he took it off, screaming, "Leave me alone!" He threw it and hit shorty with it. I met him with the ball.

"Hey, man, I'm Lewis."

"I'm Tommy. Lewis, I'm gonna kill that bastard. He's my stepdad.

"This bastard tells me, go right, I will go left. I was taking a nap on the couch. I look up, the bastard had his hand in my little sister pants. Mom did not believe me. That's what hurt. She blame me for starting trouble, said, I don't like him because of my dad. She took this bastard side because he's rich and buy things my dad cannot afford. I'm gonna kill him."

"Man, you keep saying this. Ya gonna convince yourself to do it and go to prison. Who gonna take care of ya family? Tommy, ya look like your mother. You do not want to go to prison looking like her. Looking like ya stepdad, I will say go ahead. Nobody gonna bother ya in there." We laughed. "My street ball name is Clang. Yours is Too-tall."

"I like it, Clang!"

"Well, we are gonna chitchat all day or play ball? Too-tall, one last thang. It's somebody I want ya to meet, okay?"

"Okay, Clang."

My friends were playing timid ball until Officer Poe drove up, got out the car, sat on the hood. He began punching the air saying, "Way to go," using our street ball names. We never told him our street ball names. Now I knew he was talking to the other kids about us. The porch people saw his carryings-on. They slowly went into the house. Gleaming eyes, my friends began showing off. They began imitating the best basketball player in the world. I came to the conclusion quickly: stop this madness before they blow up. I marveled at the way they shot with confidence. They stepped it up to get the blessing of Officer Poe. A first, "Hey y'all, let's give Officer Poe some respect." He always called us over.

"Well, I see for myself great sportsmanship, so I will not ask about cursing or fighting. Y'all have something I need to know about?" The usually response no sir! He turned toward the car, assuming the answer, knowing we never confided in the police. It's embedded in Negroes at an early age. Fear the establishment, police your own.

I said, "Yes sir!" He was still moving. Hit him like a ton of bricks. Another first. He turned back, all eyes on me. The black kid's nonverbal expression was laughable.

"Clang, we do not do this! What ya doing?"

"Sir, this is Tommy, and he has a problem."

"Okay, Tommy, where you live?"

"The white house with the swing."

"Tommy, I'm going to come back and arrest you, okay?"

Too-tall said, "Yeah." We shouted, "Yes, sir!" He followed suit. "Yes, sir!"

Officer Poe smiled, turned red, and for the sake of the neighborhood, said, "Y'all gonna play basketball or go to jail!"

"Basketball, sir!"

"Clang, you guys are all right."

"Too-tall, you really want to make us mad. Saying 'you guys, your kind, you people,' do not go well with us. Just say, y'all."

"Clang y'all all right."

"Yeah, man, and you Too-tall." We laughed.

"I had a good time, good-bye."

"Oh man, we only say good-bye when ya dead. We say 'c-ya.'"

"Clang, c-ya" (strangers do not get "not if I c-ya first").

"Too-tall, we can learn about each other by playing ball and having fun. One thing we have to get straight. People say we grow tails at midnight. That's a myth. That thing is not a tail." We laughed. "C-ya, Too-tall."

"C-ya, Clang."

He went into the house. Two police cars were coming from opposite directions. Blue lights on. They stopped. They went into the house and brought him out in handcuffs. (Wait a minute! How did Officer Poe know he went home? He had been watching us all the time. God, I Love This *man*. My friends did not make eye contact. I maybe said it too loud. Oh well, life went on.) The porch people came out, looking confused. He was cheering the children on. Now he came back and took the white kid away. Sadly, the Negroes were still there. A learning tool for siblings and pets. You see what happens when you play with niggers. The police will come take you away! Roof, roof, meow, meow! (Humor)

The posse slept in; nobody was on time. The wagon train did not leave until 10:30 a.m. "Since you Negroes are late, I will show no mercy on the court. Do not get offended when I manhandle ya. You are my friends, and I know something ya do not."

"What, Clang!"

"Y'all gonna be late for your own funeral."

"I hope so, Clang!" We laughed like there was no tomorrow. The porch people were not on duty. Seven kids on the court were shooting around. Too-tall came running out of the house and stopped at the gate entrance.

"Hey, Clang."

"Hey, Too-tall."

"Clang, that bastard is scared to death. I say boo, he jump. Officer Poe took me to the station, and I told him everything. I even told Officer Poe what y'all say about him. He has me repeat it. He got teary-eyed. He left to use the bathroom. Clang, I think he went and cried."

"Too-tall, you know we talk a lot. Could ya refresh my memory?"

"Remember the day I answer Office Poe with 'Yeah'? You said, 'Nobody disrespect Officer Poe, 'cause "He is The Man until The Man Comes." '(My God is amazing. I strongly believe all this happened so Officer Poe would get the message. We never told anyone directly, the messenger deliver on time. One exception, I told my cousin Mr. Haywood Hollingsworth to set the record straight. 'He is The Young Man, until The Man Comes.' I will deliver the message in the future, two white men who saved my life and The Historical President, 'You are The Man, until The Man Comes.') The family came to pick me up. They kept him for three days. We went to pick him up and he render an apology to everyone in front of the police. Now he just stay in his room, watching television."

"Did they beat him?"

"Not physical. I think this was the first time his money did not mean anything. I stayed back to play a game. My little sister and me are going to Lemon Springs to live with my dad. He's going to buy horses. Yeah man." Two females came out of his house.

"Too-tall, where are your little sister?"

"On the porch with Mom."

"Too-tall, you did not hear me. Where are your little sister?"

"Stop saying that."

"I thought a knee-high little person."

"No matter. He's the adult and should not had fonder her."

"Do not rush to judge too quickly. Mature-wise she is older than us. Too-tall, do not be overprotective. She can speak for herself, but watch her. Are we gonna talk or play ball?"

"Play ball, Clang. Here show me something." He did a quick fake to the left. I took the fake. Left-hand hook shot, swish.

"Hey y'all, Too-tall can play. I'm giving his name back! Tommy!"

"Lewis, I like my street ball name."

"I know that. Our custom we never take away. We add. Your new street ball name is Too-tall Tommy or three Ts for short. You keep hitting shots like that on the best basket baller in the world, I'm gonna call you sir." We laughed. "Y'all want to play team ball?"

"No, Clang! We saw y'all shooting the last time. We were looking out the window with our frighten parents. My dad was shaking in his boots until the police came. Let's choose. I do not want to be a loser. I want to be a winner!"

"Well, playing together while our parents are scare shitless make us winners, ain't that sumthang, Clang."

"Your name Gary, right? You have been around us for ten minutes, and we are rubbing off on ya. Thirty minutes more, I guarantee ya flunk English in school. Ain't that right!" We laughed. I put the handcuffs on three Ts, shut him down, and he was on the verge of calling me sir. His dad came in a dark blue truck.

"Clang, y'all are the greatest."

"So are y'all, man."

"Well, Clang, c-ya."

"Hey, not so fast my beautiful friend. I would like for you to show who's the better man. I notice your stepdad is helping put stuff on the truck. Hug your mom, get in the truck, drive off, stop, run back, hug your dad, forget that step shit. You are fortunate. You have two you can see. We have three we can feel but not see. I'll explain it to you later. Meanwhile your new dad looks beat down. Man, depression kills."

"Okay, Clang, c-ya."

"Yeah, man, c-ya." Three Ts followed the script. His dad hugged him a long time and cried like a baby. Younger sister ran back. His mom, all huddled, all cried. I realized this family leaving brought them together (I mumbled, "Damn! If I was only white I could be a movie director."). I had to shoot baskets. I got emotional, and a farce in my childhood—real men did not cry.

"Y'all coming next Saturday?"

"Officer Poe did not come by and check on us. So we have the green light to come any day."

"Okay, y'all, c-ya."

"Yeah, man, c-ya. Gary, tell ya old man the greatest fear is fear itself. We came in peace. We will leave in peace."

"Okay, Clang."

Bland's Drugstore was the center point for both playgrounds. After playing, we ended up there for refreshment and boasted about plays, moves, shots made, blocks and things that occurred, good or bad. (Mr.) Jimmy Bethune came across the tracks very excitedly.

"Clang, y'all not over there. We have taken over."

"Fighting or cursing?"

"Naw, Clang, we cool!"

"Y'all playing team ball?"

"We choose sides, and I always take the little white kid, Monte. He' deadly, do not miss."

"Yeah, he told me why. He is little and shoot misses he does not play. Jimmy Monte little, but he's old folks." We laughed.

"Guess who says, 'I'm Clang.' My brother (Mr.) George (Bethune)."

"You tell that little left-handed rascal he better live up to the hype if he gonna be me, the world greatest. He does not I'm coming to see him, and I'm not gonna be happy. Do Officer Poe come by?"

"Sometimes."

"Well, he must see good sportsmanship. If he stop and get out of his car, everyone go pay respect, okay?"

"Okay, Clang."

"'Cause he gave us permission to play in the white neighborhood, and the saying goes, 'He is The Man, until The Man Comes.' Jimmy those words just flowed like an act of God. Like now we are 'Here for a Reason,' and it came to me again. Tell all the guys who have caring fathers taking care of family business, and your dad is the best, Mr. Eddie Bethune. Out of respect for your dads say, 'I heard He is The Man, until The Man Comes.' Okay?"

"Okay, Clang!"

"Your mom and dad coming to the hog head party?"

"Mom for sure!"

"Well, I hope they both come. They tell stories, changing storytellers, not missing a beat. We look like people at a tennis match. (They are the real *Honeymooners* and more funnier.) They sack each other up, and your dad made history. The only person to sack someone without talking. Your mama said, 'You children make us feel old.' Everybody knows your mama's sisters. I'm tired of all the aunts. A stranger walk in, look around, he would think we are all brothers and sisters. We wanted children now to hot to wait. She is right the mothers looked so young. All the children line up for a bop (hit) "(baptize with a role of newspaper) on the head, you will cut out the aunts! All the children got a tap. I overacted and got some laughs by falling down. Then she gave your dad a wop (big hit). Mama said, 'Elsie, why you wop Eddie?' 'Well, he's not housebroken yet!' Your dad get up, went to the corner, sniff, turn around, acting like a dog. Raise his leg like urinating, looking back, wagging his tongue. The house went up with laughter. Your mother was crying, laughing, and felled on the floor. Story-telling time she stayed in the kitchen while doing her part. She could not look at your dad without laughing. I hope they come. They are the life of the party. I do not have to perform for everybody. The grown-ups do their thang. I take on Doris Jean and the little people. They laugh just to be laughing."

"Okay, Clang, c-ya."

"Not if I c-ya first, c-ya, Jimmy!"

(Recently I went through the neighborhoods after many years. People black, white, Hispanic are living in harmony. The goals still have nylon nets. The school is now the Salvation Army. I marveled at the small size of the court now; also, the distance traveled by children of color under the protection of God and a man who only saw children. This was ideally foremost greater than one step for man, a giant step for tearing down "racism.")

"Lewis, Cille home?"

"Naw, Mama went over Carrie Lee to help with the hog head party."

"I went over to see it cooking, and I know for a fact I will not be eating that. Lewis, I am gonna tell ya somethang. 'Pay back is a motherfucker!' Old black Mac came in the poolroom not in uniform. He had on a gray sport coat with a big bulge on his right hip, letting us know he has a gun. 'Hi y'all doing?' Nobody speak. I heard the talking and laughing. 'What stop ya, the police!' Walking to the front counter where Mr. John Robinson stood, he turned and shouted, "Y'all listen here! I heard a white policeman being coming here bothering Negro children. I want to know why. We know white men don't do anythang for Negroes, especially young Negro boys unless they got a thang for them and gonna get them in a whole lot of trouble! I'm gonna put a stop to this 'fore somethang happens! I'm reaching out to ya to help save our children!' Lewis, I think he is jealous of the white policeman. The white policeman got something he will never get from the black community, respect. I guessed he's worry how he would be look at by Chief and other policemen, and he's taking it personal. (Writing my memoirs: "Too-tall" Tommy, a white kid, delivered the message at the police station concerning how black children loved, respected, and admired a white policeman. Old black Mac got his information from within the police station, not from the streets and he was shamefaced!) He shouted, 'We need to put a stop to this! What do ya say?' He looked at Mr. John Robinson 'cause no one else made eye contact with him.

"We pretended he's not there, a sign of disrespect. 'Mac, we grew up together, fishing, working, and such. We known each other a long time,' and John Robinson says, 'Don't stir up stuff. It might stink!' We laughed. Foreseen also as disrespect. 'Since he has taken our children under his wings, I don't have to corral anyone for cussing. Mac, if that white man walk in here now, I will be first of many to stand in line, shake his hand, and say, "Thank you. The greatest honor our children give ya. They call ya name and say, 'You are The Man, until The Man Comes.'" The message is delivered, and a lot of men here are waiting on the postman and the white policeman.' 'Well, John, I think we should stop this foolishness.' 'Mac, you are on your own. I witness nobody here with ya. You are not speaking for us, and one thang I know ya are not.' 'That's a liar!' Lewis, Gene Knight make eye contact and say, 'What the children say?' The person used the saying. Old black Mac could not take it. He shouted, 'Trick, you better stop! You remember the last time we tangle?' 'Sir, I cannot forget. Each day I see these scars on my face, reminds me how I was snatch off the street, handcuff hands in the back, your foot on my throat, and my noggin was rung! (Remember the prelude of the beating of Mr. Gene Knight as told by Sleeping (Ugly) Beauty.) What the children say!' All the men, including Mr. John Robinson, shouted the response.

"Old black Mac got up. At the door, turn with that big gun showing. Everybody got louder. He realized he did not have enough bullets. He leaves dejected. Gene never told anyone how he is scared and by whom. (Old black Mac flunky, Ed Sleeping Beauty Dixon spill the beans. He was beat because his girlfriend was a married woman.) Everything quiet down, and a man who never talk, Mr. William Black, got up and shouted, 'Pay back is a motherfucker!' The men start chanting, imitating old black Mac actions at the door with the gun. Since a silent man spoke up, Mr. John Robinson let it continue. He asked, 'Where the children get this?' I told them, you. Mr. John Robinson said, 'I shoulda known it's Lewis.' You ready to go? The poolroom family want to see ya."

"Beau-friend, I really don't wanna. I know who's sticking his hand thru the fan, stealing his peanuts. I think he knows too." He filled the jar every night and said, "Maybe this is all they have to eat," and he has cases. We walked in. The men were grinning and facing the wall. Beau-friend turned to the left and faced the wall, also grinning.

Mr. John Robinson said, "Come up front, Lewis." On the counter were a jug of Roma Rocket wine and the smallest cup I had ever seen. He poured and turned his back. I drank the wine. I had been trying to get a whig (drink) for years. Always got caught, somebody always watching would give the signal to my brother, caught. Ahhh. Mr. John Robinson turned back.

"Another shot please, Mr. Bartender."

The men turned, laughing, and Beau-friend said, "Oh hell, no! Lucille McLean not gonna kill me! Lewis, get your ass home!"

One day, I took money out of my money drawer, put it in a brown bag, and gave to the culprit with instructions. "Walk in the poolroom, give the bag to Mr. John Robinson, turn, and leave." Beau-friend told him I knew the mouse who was taking the peanuts. The family called the guilty party a mouse. The mouse did what I said. As he turned to walk away, Mr. John Robinson called him back and gave him a box of peanuts. He said, "Give Lewis his or our money back and tell him, 'Nice try.'" You had to get up early in order to fool Mr. John Robinson. By the way he has a beautiful daughter, Ms. Barbara.

(The shelter will have a basketball court named Officer Poe Complex. Chain and nylon nets. The glass back boards will have his picture encased. I called the police station, hoping to get a picture. I will go with a copy of the book or excerpt. I will put forth Officer Poe as I saw him, positively. A man ahead of time. The hood grapevine stated him as saying, "Build the children a park, or they will play in your neighborhood.")

Mr. John Robinson said, "It's taken us over ten years fighting racist City Hall, but I envision the children will have a park next year." He took the kids to the white neighborhoods to play, and those white people did not like or want this. Allowing children equal treatment under the law made the racist city manager concede, and a park was built. The park was separate and not equal. The black community concept—a little something is better than a whole lot of nothing, and we had enough of "nothing."

The poolroom family who did not support old black Mac's scheme to condemn a fair and just man, the title "Mister" is warranted on all: John Robinson, Henry Lee McLean, Ishmael Buf'fin, Eugene Knight, Bobby Knight, Henry Smith, Dave Smith, Harry Smith, Tick Johnson, Bobby Johnson, Tom Wilson, Topsy, William Black,

Bro Ditty Smith, Chinch Davis, Eddie Davis, James Jackson, Benny Lee Smith, Richard McIver, Charlie Floyd, Charles Purcell, Monk Allen, Andy Purcell, C. B. Addams, Willie Hooker, Marion Bland, Willie Blue, Allen Baker, Wimpy McLean, Donny Berryman, Jimmy Berryman, Crybaby McLeod, James McLean, Bobby Martin, Droopy Martin, Jessie McLeod, Paul McLeod, Slyvester Turner (first Washington (slave owner) Park director), Herman Martin, Herman McLean, Aldo McLaughlin, Donny Smith, Charlie Blue, De'berry Southerland, Billie Marsh, John Marsh, Snap Moore, Peanut Shaw, Chamberlain (Stilt) Millhouse, Herbert Siler, Glenn Snipes, John Henry Johnson, Larry Taylor, Benny Lee McLeod, Charles Cotton, Richard Hammer, John Willie Hammer, Sargent Sammy Best (Special Forces, lost his life in Viet Nam, a professional drummer), and the men I cannot recall now: "You Are The Man, until The Man Comes!"

Mr. W. Marshall
Physical Education

(Superman)

Lacy McLean (Pop)

CHAPTER 5

David, You Got Balls

After Beau-friend's body slammed me on the court, the goal came down. God put another man in our life. I had a ball and a place to play; our brother relationship became stranded. In his eyes, I was the one to be blamed and be punished. "You do not have time for me, you do not have time for my money."

"I have pride." I would ask him for money only over my dead body. Our group at Bland's Drugstore was talking about making our own money. (Mr.) Junior Smith walked up.

"What y'all up to?"

"Nothing much!"

"I tried to catch y'all up here. Thought ya might want some of this." He pulled out a wad of cash and flashed it. "Lewis, you are big enough to carry golf bags and can make this." Found out later that his attention tool was a fake. Couple dollars with paper. "All y'all want some of this? Be here Saturday morning at eight o'clock." He had us hooked like a fish on a line.

The road to the golf course was dangerous and longer than the railroad. Never go by yourself. White people played a game of chicken. Chased you with their cars with horns blasting. They chased you to the woods line. They laughed. We did not get the humor. Stupid bravery—hit by the car; you should play Russian Roulette with a loaded gun. No medical treatment or transportation was available for Negroes. The most heinous confrontation involved children. A white lady driving a white station wagon filled with cub scouts in new-looking uniforms kept turning around, trying to run us over. She lost control and came within a foot of hitting a tree. I said, "Thank you, Jesus," for them, mostly for us. The white lady's word would have been taken as true. Our lives would have been altered or destroyed by this evil person. The cubbies were crying, screaming for her to stop. Hitting the steering wheel, she was yelling, "Shut up! Shut up now before I kill ya all! It's just a buncha of niggers, so shut up!"

"Hey, (Mr.) JT (Smith), where is Junior and them?"

"I don't know, think they left already. They were at Oddfellow Masonic Hall, throwing at pigeons."

"Let's catch them!" The holdup point was the florist shop's parking lot off Main Street. Negroes working at the Colon brickyard would give us a ride. A first, fat white man stopped. "Y'all going to the golf course?"

"Yes, sir!"

"Well, hop in. I'm going by there." He had on the attire of a businessman: black suit, white shirt, no tie or hat. "Y'all want to see some pictures?"

JT was in the middle, pictures were put on his chest without waiting for a response. Naked white women. While looking at the pictures, the fat man had a newspaper on his lap. His left hand was under the paper and was moving. "Sir, will you please stop? I'm about to pee on myself."

"Y'all don't piss in my car. Guess the picture got to you. It has that effect on you." Getting out, I pulled JT's pants, and he followed me into the wood line. We went a safe distance and watched the fat man. He got out and looked in the woods and closed the door uttering a curse word, using the Lord's name in vain. He kept turning around; we stayed in the woods.

"JT, we have to tell everybody about that sick bastard."

"Yeah, Lewis, the paper was moving. He was playing with himself." We passed the word and vowed stay in a group; it was more safe.

Coming back was another ordeal. Going to the golf course on the road grown-ups. Returning on the railroad children. The road curved and the railroad was straight—faster time when walking. Prior to town on the right side, there was a large wooden house, supposed to be white. Peeling paint made it look rusty blue. Never had I seen grown-ups' lights on and children with coats or shoes. The children looked mousey, except one who was fat. We gave them the name Spank and our gang. The children were brave. They would come to the railroad bank about ten feet and call names.

"Hi, ya nigger, hey niggers came from our gang." Spank was a gem diamond in poverty. He said the word "nigger" sounding like a parrot voicing in three stanza. I am sure Spank's ancestors gave him a standing ovation when he belted out the word "nigger" in hell. After an encounter, I suggested stockpiling rocks for the next day. Same routine. "Everybody throw at Spank, not the children." Rocks rained down on Spank; he was crying for our mercy. One rock hit his left forearm, made a gash with blood. We ran and stayed away from the railroad for a while. (Mr.) Donny Ray Tyson said Spank was no more. Our gang stayed on the porch. The tall girl was the new leader and still called us niggers. One kid in red plaid shirt, maybe immobile, sat in the window and warned tall girl and our gang, "Niggers on the tracks." We carried white people's golf bags and were called caddies. We picked up buckets of balls that were hit for thirty-five cent per bucket—called "shaggin." (Today in my favorite radio program *Little known Black History Facts* recognition is given to the master caddie, Mr. (Skillet) Johnson. He has been a caddie and has been "shaggin" balls for over fifty years. Tom, the word is racist!) White men loved the term and would use it anytime. "Hey, y'all shaggin! What so funny! Where is the buckets of balls?" I sat on the ground, scraped an area with a stick, and wrote the word. My eyes opened. On reversing the word, I realized what we were called. I stopped and gave a lame excuse when asked. I suggested, "Let the younger kids do this so they can make money and stop playing so much."

We had a secret. Go early, play golf. Junior Smith was the best golfer ever. He played to surprise and get laughs. "Lewis, the ball is gonna hit the tree on the right, then tree on left, then tree on right on the green, might go in the hole." Junior just take a wedge (golf club) and go over the trees. "Lewis, I'm gonna teach you somethang about golf and life. It's your thang (thing). Do what you want to do. Don't let people tell ya who to socket to." We laughed. He would pull off the feat and watch your face. He had the same laugh now as before Santa—"Ho! Ho! Ho!" It came from the stomach, and he would say, "Oh, yea of little faith."

A man surveying told Pro he saw niggers playing golf. He gave us a warning. "If you are caught playing on the course, you will go to jail!" Carrie Lee's (Big Mama) older son managed the course. "Hey, Lewis."

"Hey, Haywood."

"Lewis, ya want a job?"

"Yep!"

"You not gonna ask how much it pays?" Haywood had been out the hood too long; this was a sign of disrespect.

"Haywood, a little bit of something better than a whole lot of nothing. Cuz (cousin) I had my fair share of nothing."

"Well, Pro pays me seventeen dollars every other day. I will give ya seven dollars. You take care of the greens (area holes are), anythang I tell ya. I will be ya boss (remember he said 'boss' first). How about it?"

"Okay, cuz, shake."

Now I got a chance to play golf, so I hid clubs in the woods. My confidence club was the six iron called my six-shooter. I did not know the fundamentals of golfing, just simply put my second shot will be the six-shooter. Man this game was too easy. Pro said, "Do not water the greens at night."

I worked for Haywood. Night was when I practiced putting. What you do in the dark, you can do better in the light. At night I would put two flashlights down putt close and study. Turn lights off and putt from memory. The greens had brown-and-whitish spots from lack of watering and cutting too close. Following Haywood's guidelines the greens were becoming beautiful. Thank you, God! People noticed and let it be known what a good job Pro was doing. Haywood was my boss, and Pro did not like it. With me standing there, he did not see me over two weeks.

"Haywood, you went over my head, but this boy (word to belittle Negro males. An eighty-year-old black man was called boy, no matter your age. Nigger, boy, and the new trend is to call an eighty-year-old black man, young man) will come to me for pay!" Haywood ran the golf course. Pro was an alcoholic stooge and knew Haywood was important. He downplayed the circumstances; without Haywood, no Pro. People were making positive comments about the course, particularly the greens. Pro was taking the overall credit; we were transparent. A group of his ass-wipes were admiring the course. Now was his chance to make people believe the hype. He did this, not God. "Boy, did ya water the greens today (water at night the greens, will be soaked, and people would complain)?"

"No, sir!"

"Why not!"

"Haywood says not to. It's gonna rain." The chance was worth waiting for to show his dealings firsthand.

He yelled, "Robert (wow, he knew my name), Haywood no damn weatherman! How he know if it gonna rain or not?" Looking at his ass-wipes, he said, "Now I will have to give him a raise for forecasting the damn weather! What the hell he know! Not a cloud in the sky" God turned on the shower. The ass-wipes were laughing, holding each other up and pointing at Pro. I ran to the refreshment shed and looked back. He was standing, looking stunned in the rain. Finally, when the rain slowed, three men talked him into getting out and going on the porch. My God is a show-off. God the Father against you, who can stand for you (Jesus). One of my mother's sayings fits well here. "God don't like ugly!" Pro never contradicted Haywood's judgment again. I never told anyone of this divine gesture. Haywood will have to read my memoir. I know he will. I mentioned a part of his anatomy that makes him proud.

A man stood out while Pro and his ass-wipes were sticking fingers in butts and grabbing penis. This is called grab ass. He was called Doc, and he did not participate in the reindeer games. He rarely talked, but, when he did everyone listened. He walked up to me out of the clear blue and said, "Thanks."

"You are welcome, Doc."

"You do not hear thanks from white people too often, do you?" (I did not want to kill the moment by saying, "Not often, you are the first.")

"No, sir!"

"That's a damn shame."

Doc was cool, calm, and collected. Today the three Cs are combined into one word "articulate." President Barack H. Obama would be Doctor (Doc) Watson.

There was no brotherly love; the middle son, Billy, wanted to appease his close-minded father. He told his mother that Haywood and Jay drank beer and Jay was acting like (a) Haywood. He violated his dad's rules when it came to those people. Pro had an alcohol abuse problem, so his mother came out to rectify the problem. She was a stout woman who never spoke, just smiled. Jay was kicking footballs barefoot. She made him come in through the back door. Customers were up front; he walked past her. She snatched him around and screamed, "Before I let you ruin your life, become a drunk like your father, I will kill you! You hear me!"

"Yes, Mom, sorry!"

Haywood intervened. Which reminds me of a slave episode. The mansion was on fire. "Master! Master! Come quick! Our house on fire!"

"Haywood, did you open his mouth and pour the beer down his throat?"

"No, ma'am."

"Haywood, he takes full responsibility, you understand?"

"Yes, ma'am." She corralled Pro. Jay started kicking booming kicks again, barefooted, and was letting off steam.

"Every time you kick, my foot hurts."

"Robert, I am not using my toes, kicking on the side of my foot."

"I understand that. Still my foot hurts. Your foot okay?"

"Yeah, Robert, the foot okay. I am going to ask coach can I kick barefoot next year. I cannot stay overnight for a while, and I have some making up to do for my mother."

"You will just remember something and do not forget mothers are special."

"Thanks, Robert."

"No charge."

"Lewis, I got Jay in trouble."

"Haywood, you are more of a father figure than Pro. Don't beat yourself up. Use better judgment when Billy around, he will do anything to gain attention from Pro. You gonna stay overnight? Pro wants one of us to watch the beer and whiskey. They are having a party tomorrow. They drink all day. At night, the ladies get naked and run through the water sprinkler. That's why Pro want ya to leave."

I left and came back. I sat in the woods and watched. "Cuz, I saw a lot of tits and asses. One lady lay down on the grass and went to sleep. They stayed on the balcony. If not, I was gonna drag her in the woods and fuck her."

"Cuz, peeping at shit like that, you are gonna go blind." We laughed.

Pro and his baby son David walked up. Haywood said, "Robert gonna stay out tonight."

"Dad, can I stay out?"

He asked three times before Pro answered, "Yeah."

I took a birdbath. No showers, just a tub. Brushed my teeth and came back to the community room. David was in bed; he said, "Robert, I'm not suppose to sleep with your kind."

"Okay, first go, wash and brush your teeth."

"I don't have a toothbrush."

"Well, ya not using mine! Go wash your hand. I will put some on ya finger. Since you not suppose to sleep with my kind, you can get on the floor, Haywood bed (the pool table), or the couch. Now do what I say."

When he got back, I had put the couch cushion on the bed. One side was three feet, the other side was one foot. "David, I made the bed separate but equal."

"Robert, it's separate but not equal."

"I'm gonna teach ya a new word. It's 'why.'"

"Robert, I know that word."

"Well, then use it? I'm gonna show you how to use the new word I taught you. Why is it separate but not equal?"

"Your size is bigger than mine."

"David, you are white, so the big side is yours. Now it's okay?"

"No, Robert, it's still not equal."

"Well, fix it, little blond-head boy." We laughed.

"Robert, you beat me playing pool and cards. I know something I can beat you at."

"What?"

"Golf, because your kind do not know how to play."

"When people tell you something, use the new word I taught you."

"Robert, why your kind do not know how to play golf?"

"We are not allowed! Do you understand? We are not allowed! Your dad said, if we are caught on the course we will go to jail. Jail do not bother me. It's Sheriff Holder breath feared by all Negroes. His breath is more dangerous than his gun." David laughed. This little blond-headed boy was smart and I was going to challenge him to have an open mind, and he listened, learned, and laughed easy. When I woke up, he had moved the cushion. Lying with his left arm hugging me. The little blond-headed boy forgot the line of separation while he slept.

People started arriving early. I had to wait for Pro to pay me. I did not have this problem with Haywood. It seemed Pro waited for you to ask. I didn't have a problem asking. I had worked for it. This was a drinking party. Everybody had a glass and kept pouring. These were not wives, I deemed, party ladies. Some ladies would come on the balcony, look around, and wave to get your attention. They raised their shirt or blouse, showed you their bras, then laughed. One lady would call you, "Boy, come get my bags, take to the first tee." Get to her car, dress up (will tell you why later), no panties. Haywood made it his business to get her bags. "Cuz, you gonna go blind one day."

The men on the balcony played grab ass, excluding Doc. David walked toward me, pulling his golf cart with a big smile, like he knew something I didn't. "Robert, you want to play golf?"

"David, I told you about Sheriff Holder. He got ten kills under his belt. You want me to be number eleven? And I will tell ya a secret only Negroes know. Sheriff Holder got ten notches on his gun handle and never fired his weapon." He laughed.

"Robert, my dad says, you can play. Yeah right. I used the new word. 'Why Robert not allow to play golf? I want to play. Why Robert can't play. Why?' He says, 'Tell Robert he can play.'"

"David, I will use your new word. Why you want me dead?"

Looking at me, he shouted, "Dad!"

"What!"

"Didn't you say Robert can play?"

"Yeah, Robert, you can play!"

"Darn, you did use the word I taught ya." He did not win in pool or cards. He believed the close-minded hype from someone he trusted and loved. David wanted to prove his dad's way of life was right. A rude awakening was justified.

"Let's start on the back side so we will finish on the front." We had two complete sets of clubs, mismatched, but we did not pay for them. People would get mad and throw clubs in the pond. In due time, we would retrieve them. David was trying to swing like a grown-up and hit the ball about thirty feet.

"David, we gonna be here all night with you trying to be a big hitter. Six tee is a dogleg left. Straight with a ninety-degree turn left (backward capital L)."

I blasted the shot. "Wow, Robert, I didn't know you could do that."

"David, you are young. Lots of stuff you do not know." Next shot was six iron six inches from the hole.

"Robert, I . . ."

"Do not say it, David. I know! David, eighth shot make the green about fifteen feet from the hole. David, you play my ball and do not miss."

"Robert, I can't miss this." Overconfident, he almost missed. We laughed. "How would you play this shot?"

"Putt, close, two-putt. David, always putt to make it."

"I do not like to two-putt. It look like somebody took scissors, cut a path to the hole (call a line), put the ball on the path with enough speed. It goes in the hole." I made the shot. "Lord," I said again, "this game too easy!"

"Wow, Robert! Robert, I want to watch you play. I will keep score, and you play two balls."

"Let's get this right. I have two balls, and you do not have any."

"Robert, I got balls."

"The new word, 'why' you think you have balls and not dingle berries?"

Laughing, he said, "Robert, I got balls."

"Do not stare with those blue eyes. I can read your child mine trying to come back with your new word. I do not know what dingle berries are, either." We laughed.

"Robert, how you know I was thinking that?"

"Easy! When I was your age, I used your new word a lot."

He ran to me with a hug like Granny; I did not know what to do with my hands. I hugged him back. "David, we do not hug. Make a fist." I made a fist. "Now touch. That's how we hug, got it?"

"Yeah, Robert!"

"You are staring again, so I will answer the new word, 'why' we do not hug. Your case, your dad will punish you for hugging my kind. (My first hug from a white person, and I had to suppress the incident.) Let's play golf. The lower score put under your name."

I was playing golf, not looking to run. I was relaxed and had permission. My mind-set was that I will prove to David, Negroes can not only play with opportunities, they can be exceptional. I don't want nobody to give me nothing. Just open up the door; I will get it myself (Thank you, Mr. James Brown, "Godfather of Soul").

"Three-foot putt. David, watch." I closed my eyes, turned my head to the right, and made the putt.

"Robert, *wow!*"

Any putt six inches or less, he putt and marked the scores with a big grin. The smaller the score, bigger the grin. The fourth hole was dogleg right. Straight down ninety degrees right. "David, go down to the big oak tree that's sticking out Stand behind it so I will not hit you." It took him a long time, he had every golf club made. "David, look behind you. Can you see the greens?"

"Yeah."

"Okay, let me know where the ball goes."

I blasted over the oak tree. "Robert! It's on the green!"

149

"Okay, watch this one."

"It's on the green too. Wow!"

This feat was shown to me by the greatest golfer who played clown golf, knowing the color of his skin was a hindrance to his playing, Mr. Junior Smith. I made two's by which par is four, if you play conventional. The fifth hole ended in front of the clubhouse. Pro and his ass-wipes were still on the balcony, drinking and playing grab ass, excluding Doc.

"David, I'm playing one ball. I do not want your father knowing I can play golf, okay?" He did not answer. I assume (make ass-u-me) he got the message. Second shot—two feet from the hole.

"Robert, I will give you that. I saw you make shots like that with your eyes closed."

"Get the ball, and I had fun." David had gone mute on the last hole. He got the ball, annotated the score, dropped his golf cart, and waving the card and screaming, he ran to the clubhouse. I put the community clubs away and went to the Coke machine. Pro and thirty-odd men confronted me. Doc put David in a golf cart, breathing in a bag.

Pro said, "Robert, you shoot these scores?"

"Yes, sir."

"These are some mighty fine scores. Mind if we see ya hit some?"

"No, sir!" Number one hole was tailor-made for my six-shooter.

Pro handed a ball. I put it six inches left of the hole. He tossed the next ball. "Let me see ya do that again." Six inches in front of the hole.

A man said, "I haven't seen a swing that sweet since Bobby Jones" (I did not know Bobby Jones). Another man said, "Only if this boy was white think of the money we could make."

He tossed the ball at my feet. "Let me see ya do that again" (hint—confidence club, I could do this all year). Shot six inches right of the hole.

David took the bag down and said, "Didn't I tell y'all Robert is the best golfer in the world?"

Doc told him to breathe in the bag. He took it down again. "Robert, show them the spin shot."

Pro threw the ball at my feet. I noticed the color in his face change from alcohol red to pale, with a large gray vein protruding on the left side of his neck. "Yeah, Robert, let us see the spin shot."

The men turned heads while laughing at Pro's conduct. I will not take credit for this shot. Mr. Junior Smith taught it to me. Guideline given to me: "Lewis, the key is the tee" (invented by a black man who would not be allowed to play on most golf courses)! The ball spun back, went in the hole.

David screamed, "Told ya, Doc, Robert is better than my dad!" The ladies came on the balcony to see what the men were doing.

One lady shouted, "Oui, Wee. That boy hitting that ball really turn me on!"

The lady holding her knees to keep her from falling over the rail said, "Mabel, anything turns you on." The men laughed; all eyes were on me. I did not laugh along with Doc and Pro.

David was shouting, "Robert, can I putt those in! Can I, Robert?" We had a secret—something not important, I would call him Dave. "Okay, Dave."

"Let's go, Doc. Robert say I can putt those in. Doc, I told you Robert is better than my dad!" The ass-wipes respected Pro by turning away while laughing.

"I haven't seen a swing that sweet since Bobby Jones" (I did not know Bobby Jones). On cue, "Only if this boy was white think of the money we could make." The prejudice melee Pro instilled in his sons were a farce. David in front of white people was saying that a black person was the better golfer. Out of the mouth of babes comes the truth. Also in front of white people, it was a first. Out of the mouth of a drunk loose woman comes the truth. Ms. Mabel was Pro's mistress who took golf lessons. "Y'all listen up. When I'm conducting golf lesson on the backside, do not come back there." He walked away.

"Cuz, did I hear Pro right, he want us back there when he's giving lesson?"

"Haywood, I did not hear that."

"Well, I'm going to see why. You coming?"

"Naw, you go ahead."

On returning, he said, "Lewis (usually if given name is called, truth follows), you want to know why?"

I did not waste my breath. Haywood was going to tell anyway. "That lady on her knees sucking his limp dick. He drink so much whiskey, dick will not get hard. I started to say, 'Pro, you need some help. Let her lick on Mr. Johnson. He's too big for her mouth.' Cuz (usually bullshit follows), I walk out of the woods knocking over trees with my dick."

"Little trees!"

"Naw, cuz, big damn trees. All I needed was a blue ox, and I would hava been call Paul Bunyan." We laughed.

"Robert, that's some mighty fine hitting. Come on, I'm gonna buy you a Coke." I reached for the Coke; he held on and got my attention. With those cold green eyes, he said, "Nigger, you leave this place and don't ever come back!"

"Pro, you owe me seven dollars." He gave me ten dollars from the pocket of his pinkish white shirt and walked away. I did not take his final gesture to heart—a tip after he gave me his one and only best shot. I dropped three dollars by the Coke.

My first real job and I lost it for showing off. Who could I blame? Me! After all these years, I had not learned my place. Natural abilities did not count unless you were white. "A swing like Mr. Bobby Jones" (I did not know Bobby Jones) did not matter. "Only if this boy was white, think of the money we could make."

I had to leave his premises. If I dared to go on the road by myself, it would be suicidal. I wondered if the Den Mother gave the cubbies merit badges for saving their lives. I looked back. Pro had gone back and picked up the money and was drinking the Coke. He was stalling. I would not like to be in his shoes, preaching a way of life that was proven flawed by his own hands. Asked why Robert could not play, he should stick to his guns. "Golf is for white people only. It's a thinking man game. Niggers cannot think, and they stink up our way of life. We will protect until death do apart. That boy cannot play!" He had nowhere to hide; he had to face facts. A Negro shot the lowest scores ever on this course, playing two balls. Choices were hard to make, especially when your life was on the line. The railroad was also dangerous; however, hiding in the woods, if you got caught, you would be at the mercy of Sheriff Holder's deadly breath. He had ten notches for ten kills on his gun's handle and never fired his weapon. I decided I will take the railroad.

In remembrance, I looked at the beautiful grass God made and I maintained. I had to urinate, and I would not do it on God's creation. A new lawn mower Haywood and Pro assembled without using the Instructions. (A terrible mind should be wasted.) After completion, the gas mower ran on oil. There was a hole over the oil housing. Haywood came to the conclusion that it was made for a Pepsi bottle, perfect fit, not Coke. The bottle had a little oil in it. I urinated and placed it back down.

On the railroad tracks, I got two bricks and walked. I had a pocketful of money. If confronted, I would fight and needed my energy. We usually ran until we got to the clearing which housed "our gang." I got to the clearance, bricks in hands. I looked at the children who were on the porch. "I will not tolerate being call a nigger again today. I will throw at the upper level, not hit the children, they are innocent. However, an adult come out, man, only I will throw at him." The look in my eyes, the bricks in my hands, or both said, "Do not fuck with me." There was not a sound from the children.

Next day, Haywood came to the house. "Hey, Lewis (usually no bullshit), what's up? Pro wants to see ya. Want to know if ya put water in the new mower."

"Naw, man, I did not put water in the mower. Tell Pro taste. It's probably nigger piss. Before ya ask, I did not piss in the mower. I did piss in the Pepsi bottle."

Haywood's eyes bugged. "Oh shit! Man, get ya off the hook, tell him anything. Pro look at me with those cold green eyes and said,

'Nigger, leave this place and never come back.' Haywood, this black nigger will grant his wish, and I will never play golf again."

"Okay, Lewis, later."

"Yeah, Haywood, later" (business, no farewell with hood talk, c-yas).

Haywood was back again next day. "This must be serious. Maybe I'm truly missed. Maybe I will tell Haywood a secret about the greens—cut opposite direction, each cutting gives it the checkerboard look."

"Hey, Lewis."

"Hey, Haywood."

"Pro says will ya please come back? He will give us even money, ten dollars a day."

"Man, Pro can offer me half of his empire or John, The Baptist, on a silver platter. I will never go back or play golf again." Haywood tried a different angle, David.

"Dave crying, not eating, and accusing Pro of making you leave. He said he wants to see you play golf. 'Why Robert go! Why Robert did not bump fist! Robert say do not hug him, you will get mad. Why? You was the last one talking to Robert. Why, Dad! Why!' Pro said, 'David, you had better stop! I fired Robert. He was not doing his job!' Doc (with the zeal of the Articulate One, POTUS) spoke, 'Pro, that's not true. The light-skin boy did all the work. The black one tells him what to do then ride off on the tractor. You should have fired the black one. I have never seen this place looking like this in sixteen years.' White folks kept asking me, 'Are you the boy that got the swing like Bobby Jones?'"

"Haywood, I do not know Bobby Jones."

Robert McLean

"Cuz, I don't know that motherfucker either." We laughed. "Cuz, cars are lined all the way to the main road. Cars are parked in the woods, and I spied my white woman."

"Cuz, you better look over your shoulder when you say that. I don't want to hear they found somebody hanged and burnt beyond recognition."

"Lewis, you can tell it's me. Mr. Johnson will be dragging the ground."

"I do not think so, cuz. Mr. Johnson will be the rope used to hang your black ass."

"Now I got your attention. Cuz, do me a favor. Look before you leap."

"Okay, cuz. I woke Mr. Johnson up. Haywood, you should have let Mr. Johnson sleep, and I know why her dress is up—to keep from getting wrinkle."

"Why that, cuz?"

"A wrinkle dress will match the wrinkle squirrel. Cuz, you know why the squirrel is wrinkle?"

Naw, cuz, why?"

"Cuz, that squirrel have been busting a lot of nuts." Haywood laughed aloud.

"Cuz, ya got some. Lewis got jokes!"

"Haywood, I even know why you are always pulling on Mr. Johnson. The white man took everything from us. So, you are really checking."

"Lewis, I am not laughing at that. My worst nightmare—white folks came while asleep, put him on a truck."

"Little truck!"

"Naw, cuz, a big damn truck! They went five miles down the road before I felt the tug."

We laughed. "Five miles, cuz?"

"Cuz, you know I do ezager, ezagrate. Hell, Lewis, you know that word I'm trying to use?"

"Yeah, cuz, it's call lie!"

"Lewis, you are killing me. Mama say you are funny. I never saw this side of you."

"Haywood, when I work for you, I worked and played golf. Now I sit around all day and bullshit."

"Cuz, before I went to her car, I marvel at Mr. Johnson. He is standing attention like a soldier."

To get the full visual, I compared him with that monument in Washington DC that looked like a dick. "Lewis, You know that Jefferson Davis monument!" We laughed. "Lewis, the day Negroes learn all the tricks of the white man, it will be judgment day. White folks in Virginia know the real deal. It look like a dick because Mr. JD fucked over a lot of niggers."

"Wow, Haywood! You know your American history."

"I am changing Mr. Johnson name. He's now call Mr. JD."

"You naming him after Jefferson Davis?"

"Hell, no, Lewis. Fuck that rebel. I am naming him for the size of the monument it stands for, Mr. Jumbo Dick."

You could never be depressed with Haywood around.

"I struggled with Mr. JD and went straight to her window, dick to eye level. She could not take her eyes off Mr. JD, and she was speechless. The wrinkle squirrel mesmerized me. I strongly believe some wrinkles iron out as I watched. I was mesmerize. She is coma struck. Her breathing change and she stirred. 'Miss, would you like me to take your bag to the first tee?' All she could do, nod her head. I look at her left arm, big bumps were moving."

"Cuz, those were goose bumps."

"Cuz, I think those bumps were the goose and the fucking gander."

Now Haywood was killing me with laughter, and it felt good.

"I took her golf bag to the first tee and looked back. She had her head back, and if I was a gambling man, I bet she was ironing those wrinkles. She stayed like that until her three playing partners tap on her window. She lower the steamy window and stayed with her head back. She did not play. The three ladies watch me with a gleam in their eyes and a joyous smile. Pro checked on her and came where I am red face, raspy voice, mean look on his face, and told me go cut the fairway on number three. 'People are complaining grass too high.' The grass were playable. Pro lied. My plan went out the window with all my work. Add a courtesy for the ladies, wake up Mr. JD, and take ladies' bags to the first tee for free. Pro will not go for my plan now. He retrieve her bag and left word he wanted to see me. Doc and Pro took her home. She was too weak to fight or drive. What did he want? He ask me did I cut fairway number seven? I said, 'Yes, sir!' He was sitting at a card table with Doc, and a slew of white men looking at him. Cuz, he wanted to ask about Mr. JD but feared the aftermath of a white man asking to see a Negro dick.

I would not have objected if he requested to see Mr. Jumbo Dick. I woulda said, 'Iama (eye-ma) pulling him out with a warning. He may spit on ya, so stand back ten steps.'"

"Little steps?"

"Hell, naw, cuz, big damn giant steps." We laughed like there was no tomorrow.

"I'm in the supply room when Doc and Dave came back downstairs. They made a large scale of your scorecard. Pro in strange drunken ways tried to make amends with his son. 'Dave, are you gonna tell us how that boy made twos on number four hole?' Dave said, 'Why everybody keep saying "That boy! That boy!" His name is Robert. I don't know why you say, "That boy." His name is Robert. No! I am not gonna show you. I'm only gonna show Doc.' Doc was taking a drink. Robert said, 'He like Doc 'cause Doc got class!' Doc spit out the drink, laughing and banging fists on the table. Finally, he gain his composure and gave away his secret of not speaking out. (He sounded like the late Mr. Ted Kennedy. If you forgot how he sounded, listen to Mr. Etch a Sketch sounding of the words, not the contents.) This is the south. He has a northern accent. He said, 'I did not think I would live to see the day a Negro like a white person because he has class. As white people, we should be on our best behavior at all times. Those people are watching us as childish games or indecent conduct are displayed. We say they are inferior to us. We make laws to hindrance these people out of fear we maybe inferior to them. A white man do something, it's on him. A bad apple in the Negro race, we blame all the people. Robert carry my golf bag. Reality, the better player carry the bag, and base on ability, I would be the bag carrier.' Doc said, 'I witness Robert putting three shots six inches or less in front of the hole, and on Dave request spin shot back a hole in one. Two things I heard were colors white and green. "If this boy was white, think of the money we could make." Pro, If you made Robert leave, you cancel your blessing by your hate of Negroes. You should have put Dave, your son's feelings first. I have never seen him so happy. The greens can be compared with Augusta and never seen this many people here in sixteen years. White people should exhibit class at all times. We don't, and that's a damn shame! Let's go, Dave!' Lewis, when they got back, Doc told them what Dave said.

"Haywood, it's two messages take back for me. Tell Pro no hard feelings, and he's still the boss."

"Oh hell, no, cuz! Why you go and say that?"

"Haywood, they talk in codes, you know that. Remember Judgment Day."

"Yeah, man."

"What you think are been said? 'Hey y'all, shaggin.' Turn the word around, you have 'niggahs.' Haywood, I'm giving you the code word 'boss.' The Great Depression—stock markets crashed. Guilty people who did not stockpile money or jump off buildings, commit suicide, they went to prison. Hard currency did not disappear. Money went abroad, Swiss bank accounts. (Money inherited, never reinvented. Man seeking the highest office in the land carries this baggage.) The thieves got minimum prison time. The prison guards were call by white people, "Trash." The qualifications for a guard were simple put. Warning shots at white prisoners, shoot black nigger prisoners between the eyes. The guards were family hand-down job through generations. Majority did not know their names if written. An Ivy Leaguer resent calling people he profile as being trash, sir, or mister. He wrote many letters to the library in Washington DC. Please give him one of the large dictionary which are thrown away every five years. The library sent two and a message, "Stop." Task at hand— find a word to disgrace the guards without their knowledge. It did not take long. The word founded is 'boss.' Paragraph thirteen B stated, 'The farthest outmost portion of an erect penis.' The slang for penis is dick. What we call the tip? Head! Put the two slang together what ya have?"

"Dickhead! Wow, Lewis!"

"When a prisoner ask the guard, 'Boss, can I get a new spoon?', he say, 'Go head.' The prisoner laughs, laughs, and laughs more. The penalty for telling the guards the secret is death. I think this word is everlasting in the penal system."

"Lewis, I'm gonna call all those motherfuckers 'boss.' What about the ladies? You got a name for them?"

"Yeah, Haywood. It's mam!" he laughed.

"Lewis, you won. You are the big bull shitter (the story teller) of the day!"

"Thanks, Haywood. You still have three hundred and sixty-four left!"

"Lewis, ya are killing me!"

"Haywood, when you overburden me with work, then tack on something else, and I would say, 'Okay, boss.'"

"Lewis, you was saying, 'Okay, dickhead!'"

"Yeah, man, I'm sorry, and to show my gratitude, Haywood, 'You are The Young Man, until The Man Comes.'" (I will take the message "You are the man, until the man comes" to white men who saved my life, the historical president and a great humanitarian disk jockey.)

"Thanks, Lewis."

"Haywood, the next message is important, no bullshit. You have to be correct. David understands, if something not important, I call him 'Dave.' If you say, 'Dave, Robert said,' he's not gonna believe you. He must have gotten the smartness from his mother. He's more smart than Pro."

"Hell! Lewis, that's not saying much. Mr. Jumbo Dick is smarter than Pro, and he does not have a brain!"

"Straight up, man! Say, 'Robert said, tell David he got balls.'"

"Gotcha!"

"Hey man, (Mr.) Fatty McLeod and (Mr.) Winston Martin are going to teach me to prime tobacco. I'm paid twenty dollars a barn. We do two and half barns a day. Do the math. Haywood, thanks for hiring me. If I had to do over, I would not change a damn thang. God do not make mistakes, and 'We Are Here for a Reason.'"

"Okay, Lewis, c-ya."

"Not if I c-ya first. C-ya, Haywood."

I saw Haywood later. "Cuz, you gave David the message?"

"Sure did, the three brothers were sitting on the porch, waiting for mom to pick them up. Pro was sloppy drunk. Doc save those boys' life. Pro fell over the rail aimed for his sons. Doc grab his ankles and held on until men hoist him back up. I said, 'Dave, come here! Robert said, "Tell David he got balls." 'He made a big grin, teary eyes, and ran back in the clubhouse. Lewis, I think Pro beat that boy for not believing the venom about people because of the color of their skin. Dave saw you a better golfer than his dad, not a Negro, and Pro despised it."

"Haywood, it's a shame those white people did not see the best golfer in the world—(Mr.) Junior Smith."

"White folks are saying you are the boy with the swing."

"Hold it, Haywood! I do not know that motherfucker either! I will give credit where it's due.

(Mr. John Robinson has a beautiful daughter, (Ms.) Barbara. A crush for years. Writing my memoirs gave the reason. Wow! I do not need counseling in this matter. I only told my beautiful cousin Mrs. Agnes Hollingsworth Brooks about the crush, but not why. Here is the reason in earnest. Writing is therapy. I idolized (Mr.) Junior Smith in every way, and (Ms.) Barbara Robinson was his girlfriend.) Mom came and told Pro it will be a cold day in hell if they ever returned. She should have been talking to the big oak tree. He's in another world and piss in his pants as he fell over the balcony. The way Mom stood back as she scolded him, I think, he shit too. Haywood, let's not ridicule Pro. Let's pray for him."

"Yeah, Lewis, ya right."

"Naw, Haywood, we are both right!"

Haywood Hollingsworth (Nen'ne)

Lacy and Wanda McLean (my beautiful sister)

HONORABLE MENTIONS

1) A six iron and a bucket of golf balls were at home; I decided to get rid of the stuff. I missed playing, and the items were too enticing. I started second-guessing. I had been called "nigger" more times than my given name by white folks. (It puzzled white people who really tried to live together. Question: "How can black people call each other nigger? However, it become offensive when white people say it?") I missed seeing the little blond-haired boy and making him laugh. If Pro was serious, he should have come or trusted Haywood and let David come. Pride was too important. If I went back, it would be on my accord. "You do not stand for something you will lay down for anything" (thank you, Reverend Al Sharpton's Mother, RIP, Mother Ada Sharpton).

   I went to the short field at W. B. Wicker High School. Put the bucket downrange. Hit putting golf balls in the bucket. Professor Fisher, whom we called "Prof" came out of the building. "Robert, I had been watching you. I did not know you could do this."

   "Prof., I'm a little rusty, miss too many."

   "Robert, this is amazing." He walked away, shaking his head, turned, and said, "I wish times were different." He walked away, shaking his head. "Yes, Professor Fisher, I got the drift. If I was white, think of the money we could make." I went behind the gym and hit the balls in the woods. I leaned the club on the gym wall near the trail. "Oh God, I pray let some kid takes it. Maybe his or her offspring would be allowed to play."

2) I felt bad about the children. I was going to throw at them. Mama had fruitcakes from work. I bought fruits, nuts, candy canes, and emptied my change drawer in a giant brown paper bag. It was a warm day before Christmas; the children on the

porch were looking at me. I went halfway in the yard, placed the bag down, turned, and walked away. I looked back; the children had torn into the bag. The tall girl gave a candy cane to Mrs. Shirley Temple Black look-alike (maybe Spank's sister, chubby cheeks, was not mousey), except her curls were red. I felt good seeing the children excited and happy. I got emotional when Shirley with candy cane in her left hand, waved with her right hand. That was more than enough thanks for me. (Children like Shirley are the key to fighting racism, not old fart and the ladies of old fart. Poverty is not color blind, and I curse people who want to conserve this way of life.)

3) Many years later, I was stationed at Fort Bragg, North Carolina, with my brother Lacy, who was hitting golf balls. "Man, let me see that club a minute!" I remembered Mr. Michael Jordan in the all-star game, alone soaring for the basket, and the world waiting for something spectacular. He shocked the world— missed a dunk! The great one said, "You have to learn to laugh at yourself before you can laugh at others." I hit the ball the way I was facing, not downrange. The worst slice in the history of golf. Lacy laughed, laughed, and laughed. I laughed, laughed, and laughed. We were having too much fun. I would not spoil the fun with me pulling my chain telling this story because I really "choke!"

4) Recently I was in this metro city. I got a local newspaper and turned to the sport section. An article stated: A golf professional name Mr. David O. Sr. did not win the tournament. He made a great showing with gutsy plays. I translated the gutsy playing, "He got balls."

5) A nonwhite, Mr. "Tiger" Woods, is on top of the golf world. I am his number one fan. When he plays the final round, I also wear red. Only difference is I'm fully dressed with red shorts. I was going to name this story *Before Tiger*. I could not relate to a celebrity whom I had never seen in person. I had shared a time in my life with (Mr.) David O. Sr. In my youth, white people were scared to do the right thing. In my adult life, things

have not changed. My golf protégé (wishful thinking) had been in a hiatus (not winning) for months. I had the solution and quite obvious, your first coach was a black man. Darken your entourage and have fun. The game was too easy! Watching "Tiger" win The Arnold Palmer Invitational, a professional named Mr. Jeff O. did not change his mechanics. He hit balls in the water. Putting a six, he threw the ball in the water. He laughed at his misfortune and walked away. Damn! My eyes were playing tricks on me. Mr. Jeff O. was a replica of "Pro." (Today, my president did not change his mechanics as he bowled. A humble man I am. First time, ten consecutive strikes. The bowling alley shut down and watched me bowl. I did not know how to keep score. I did not change my mechanics, same result. I gave up trying to convince people I had never bowled before. I was referred as a natural. "Sir, look in front. You will see five arrows. Do not look downrange until you release the ball and point where you want the ball to go" (call follow through). (Task an agent responsible for your gear. Bowling alley equipment is questionable when you bowl in red states. "Those damn republicans cannot be trusted." You are a left-side one or two arrow player, by which, any pin can be played. A tidbit of a fantasy story, warning! Handshakes are for men only! Check for weapons. Hug the ladies, sir!)

Note: Racism then, now, and later. An idiot in front of the world called the leader a lie. Wars happened; this was treason. In times of war, the penalty is death. He is immediately taken from the chamber out back and shot in the head! Oh God, we owe China large sums of money. We have not taken her policies yet! God bless the president of the United States and God bless America.

Lucille H. McLean
Ms. Carrie Lee Hollingsworth (BIG MAMA)

CHAPTER 6

Tennis Will Never Be Duplicated in a Hundred Lifetimes

A summer day agenda—find the girls. I checked Washington (the slave owner) Park. I hit pay dirt. Girls everywhere and decision time. The weather was hot, but I deserved hotter. I saw it on the tennis court—(Ms.) Cleta McLeod. I overheard a statement made as I sat on the Hope Wall (explanation later); she turned back and announced to the trailing girls, "Y'all don't be late. Remember, the early bird gets the worm!" I thought, "I will be the early worm." A posted sign read, "Learn to play tennis today at 1:00 p.m." It was ten minutes before, and the girls were on the tennis/basketball courts. In the white park, the two courts were separated. The decision was made to get phone numbers. Go through the motions of learning tennis. I had my eyes on the girls, and it seemed these baby girls had eyes on a cool man. He was a math teacher, Mr. Lloyd Hoover. He was teaching basic tennis, and to keep our attention, he used the girls as demonstrators to a captive audience. I realized immediately that (Ms.) Cleta McLeod had a worshiper—(Mr.) George Owens. The other girls appeared more interested in appeasing (thank the Republican Party for this word describing our Commander in Chief. Fortitude, the black man not his plan. We the people knew sole responsibility was taken. Mission downtown Pakistan, now the great appeaser, swim with fish.) Mr. Hoover. Well, I'm not barking up a tree with nothing up there. I hit a cross-corner shot. Mr. Hoover said, "Robert, you played tennis before?"

"No, sir!"

"You are a natural. You don't teach that."

"I play ping pong pretty good!"

"Yeah, I notice you all playing three feet from the table."

"Yes, sir! We do that to impress the girls."

"Well, it's quite impressive. I want you to continue coming. I will teach you things I know."

"Okay, Mr. Hoover."

A Closing Prayer, God Bless

God Bless Very poor, poor, working poor, homeless veterans, anyone who needs a place to rest their heads.

God Bless Families who lost homes and families on the verge of losing without fault.

God Bless Culprits unlawful foreclosure after taking bail out money. God says what goes in the mouth is not dirty. What comes out is dirty. It comes from the heart. Dear God, my answer, enough is enough. Dear God, let it come from the heart, through the mouth of the guilty parties, answer to the question, How much greed is enough?

God Bless   Haves and the Have-mores (2178 plus) who do not pay a fair tax rate. Dear God, the greatest day of mankind is when you walked the earth and paid tax. Instructed the collector go to the river open the fish mouth, take the talon (money). Oh God, this 1 percent act like they are better than you, I differ. Compare, earthly might of these people could not be a pimple on the ass (donkey) you rode.

God Bless   Vice President Joe Biden and family, especially after naming his son Beau and having the fortitude to shoot people in the face with words, not a shotgun.

God Bless   President Barack H. Obama and family.

God Bless   The United States of America! *Amen.*

Mr. Hoover's rule of thumb: "Learn the basics and your overall game will come." By the third day, the girls stopped coming and so did the skinny cool brother (Mr.) George Owens. Oh well, I think they got the message he was teaching tennis only and not getting in trouble with these hot girls. He could have let us take this off his hands.

My raw talents and Mr. Hoover's teaching methods made me a kick-ass player. In six weeks, from touching a racket for the first time, I became the top player in the class. In the final week, a player came with game, Mr. Charles Marsh. He was bougie with things we lacked such as a caring father—Mr. Charles Marsh senior (made a promise and had never broken it), a beautiful home, and his own tennis gear. He was sizing the competition. After the upcoming tournament, the winner was to go play somewhere else. This was not known by us; only Mr. Hoover and (Mr.) Charles Marsh knew. He had been going representing without competition. A plan by Mr. Hoover the winner of the in-house competition would go and play. A different player, maybe different result. (Mr.) Charles Marsh played a sweet finest game. Our names were in different brackets; we played for the championship. He was winning with the bougie smile.

"Robert, you want to beat Charles?"

"Yes, sir!"

"You really want to beat him?"

"Yes, sir!"

"Play your game. You are not going to beat him playing his game. Robert, this is not you. Play your game. Power every play. Robert, power! Robert, power!"

"Okay, Mr. Hoover." He escorted him every year and knew his weakness. It worked to perfection. I wiped the bougie smile off his face. He was bougie with class. We shook hands and acknowledged great tennis. He took the first set. The next two, I won after a little birdie shouted in my ear. "Robert, you have to go play next week. Meet me here Saturday noon, okay?"

"Yes, sir!"

"I want you to practice all week. Keep the racket, and I'm giving you some fairly new balls. Those are quite dead." We laughed. The recreation parks were separate. That's all, folks (thanks Bugs Bunny, for this saying). Judge for yourself. One park have a returning wall with lights. One park's returning wall is the woods, no lights. I would go early in the morning and used the lights and the returning wall. Recreation workers saw me practicing. Next day, the court was padlocked. I saw them looking out of the top window and laughing. Instead of ranting and showing frustration, I made a solemn move. (When someone do anything vile to you, in order reverse the wrath of pain, pray for them and their evil ways. Mama's saying fits well, "God do not like ugly!") I got on my knees, hands together at my chest, and I prayed the Lord's prayer. I added, "What harm I'm doing hitting a ball against a wall?" I noticed the workers' smiles had turned upside down. The punk way out—lock the gate. He will go back to the inferior park and practice. Ideology denied access; these people will run rampant, parks, swimming pools, schools, and Lord behold, they will come to our churches. Don't they know when you die your souls are separated? I do know the latter; it's called heaven or hell.

"Mama, I do not care if I got food, clothes, or roof over my head. We need a television."

Mama came through with a warning. "Lewis, I'm not gonna forget your promise. Your butt get hungry, eat that television."

"Thanks, Mama, and I'm not saying anything stupid. So you will take it back."

There was a beautiful laugh from my mother. I was watching a rerun (edit, Negroes depicted from long range, need binoculars, sitting close) basketball game between Philadelphia and New York. The best baller from the great state of West Virginia was Mr. Hal Greer. He took over the game; he was deemed unstoppable, so the giants knocked him down. Weakness of my game would make Mr. Shaq O'Neil proud (no, insult my hero. The devil killed an angel (Ms. Shania Davis) in Fayetteville, North Carolina. Mr. O'Neil paid all expenses for the funeral. God bless Superman II).

Mr. Hal Greer went to the free throw line, bounced the ball, hit jump shots, swish, swish; he had two shots. Wow! White folks said this was a passing trend; Negroes should stick with the radio rhetoric, to be heard, not be seen. Mama chalked another one for the white folks. They are wrong again. I loved the radio and listened to games all the time. I saw firsthand that you could learn from television. Now I had to put in practice. I got my keepsake, the basketball which was given to me by a great man, Officer Poe.

Retrieved my tennis gear. At Washington (the slave owner) Park, I loosened up, shooting jump shots. Now free throws like Mr. Hal Greer. I made twenty-five consecutive free throws. A complete game, thank you, Jesus! Now shoot from the sweet spots. Areas not supposed to miss. The racket leaning on the fence was a rare miss. I knocked the racket and balls over. Overjoyed, I retrieved the items, threw the ball in the air, and jumped—ace. "Wow! A new serve. I must practice. I had a problem landing, more practice." A new day— Mr. Copycat was out of the box with the complete game and serve. I invented this with wholehearted gratitude to God and the workers who had padlocked the white people's tennis court. Nobody would know until I was ready. "I will not expose prematurely like golf. I will control my destiny. Right time, right place." Bam, boom, surprise!

We met at Washington (the slave owner) Park. "Ready to go, Robert."

"Yes, sir!" We went across town to the white people's park. We were the only black people, and Mr. Hoover kept glancing to get a reaction. I did not give him one. I trusted him with my life. He left me in the dark, maybe thinking I would be afraid of the situation, and I did not pursue the issue. He did not know I had a secret, and my only fear face an opponent with a serve like mine. The white player was showing off, so I gave him the name Mr. Show-Off. I think his racket was amplified; hits were loud. People would look at me with a smirk on their faces, and some had a look of sympathy. People's nonverbal expressions were loud and clear: "This poor boy is going to get slaughtered." "Robert, he's spending energy, showing off, may want you to extend the volleys and make him tired, okay?"

"Yes, sir!"

I went on the court to warm up and hit an easy shot over the net. Mr. Show-Off smashed it back. The people laughed loud. I looked, and he had a big shit-eating grin on his face. I exited and stood next to Mr. Hoover. "Good move, Robert, do not let him intimidate you."

"Mr. Show-Off do not sweat me, Mr. Hoover."

"Good, Robert. Now go get him!"

Mr. Show-Off, a man with whistle and clipboard, and two ladies dressed in Klan White came on my side of the net. The lady on his left was the recorder. She was tall and looked like a pencil. The lady on his right made me lie to Mr. Hoover. I sweated. She was Ms. Serena Williams, minus one beautiful asset. It appeared as if all eyes were on me. Ms. Serena is the medical advisor. I should have charged her for a checkup. Ms. Serena's legs in the short white tennis dress were like magnets. I looked away magnetized, eyes came back. Lord knows, I tried; second-stage puberty is hard (pun intended).

Mr. WC (Whistle-Clipboard) gave instructions I could not recall if my life depend on it. As the visitor I should call the toss. He looked at Mr. Show-Off call it. Head. Tail! What you gonna do? "Serve, sir!" As I was walking back to the baseline, I decided that I will release the beast, shock Mr. Hoover and the world. This time was the right time. I am in control of my destiny. Mr. Show-Off played Mr. Charles Marsh, who played a soft, sweet game. My one warm-up shot was misleading. You warm up with the opponent and fish for weak points. He played up, not knowing or getting a feel on how I played.

He said, "Are you going to hit two practice shots?"

I had not warmed up because of his showboating. "Naw, coming at you! Serving!" I threw the ball high and took two big steps, leaping high. It appeared as if I am looking down over the net. The American Flat Serve (I love the name) made contact. The ball bounced in front of Mr. Show-Off and hit him in the groin. His eyes changed. you could only see white. He dropped to his knees. Ms. Serena shouted, "Bring Ice! Towels, more ice, Ice!" People came onto the court.

Mr. WC said, "Please move back. He needs air. Please stand back!" I went to the corner where my towel and Mr. Hoover stood. It was a preplanned spot because coaching was not allowed. Decisions had to be made by the players. White folks then, now, later, believe the theory that black people can't think. Bronze without brains. Thinking handicaps blacks. That's why they will not play golf, tennis, quarterback, or be president of the United States. ("Mama, chalk up four more misconceptions.") "Robert, go tell him you are sorry this happened."

"Yes, sir." People saw me approaching and stepped aside. A sign of courtesy, or maybe I had leprosy. The injured player was in a fetal position on his right side. This was serious. I dropped the mimic name and replaced it with Injury Player. Mr. WC did not introduce us during the briefing; his ignorance was on display. Superiority was dictated by the color of your skin. I kneeled down and said, "I am sorry this happened!"

He replied in a very, very high voice, "That's okay." I got up, and for the benefit of two girls hugging, crying, and looking at me, I tapped him on the foot with my racket. "I'm very sorry." He nodded.

The ambulance was leaving. Mr. WC started clearing the court and motioned for me to come for another face-off. He started shouting, "Jeff! Jeff! Jeffrey!" This was mean-spirited, calling him out, putting Jeff on the spot. Jeffrey, sitting between two friends, stood and shouted, "Mom! Mom! I'm not gonna play him! Mom, just give him the trophy! Mom! Mom!" He ran to his mother and put his head in her bosom, crying. "Mom, I'm not playing him!"

Stroking the right side of his face, Ms. Serena looked at Mr. WC and nodded no. He threw the clipboard down and cursed the Lord's name in vain. (Puberty makes the young mind wander. Jeffrey was being consoled by his mother. I noticed she was almost a replica of the most-watched tennis player in the world, Ms. Serena Williams. Only exception was she did not have the beautiful, bodacious, make-a-man-watch-tennis-mute *smile!*) Mr. WC was a tall, skinny, black-rimmed glasses man. He gave me the impression of an expert teacher well-versed in tennis but never played the game. Mr. WC was Mr. Stokely Carmichael of tennis. Mr. SC pumped Negroes to riot while he faded out of the picture. A Negro had never won the tournament. He should have played in order to keep the record intact (wishful thinking my serve is life-threatening). Like Mr. SC, Mr. WC wanted someone else to do the dirty work. He also displayed a likeness to Mr. SC called "chicken shit!"

"Robert, are you ready to go?"

"Yes, sir!" We got to the car; Mr. WC came running with the trophy.

"Here ya are for winning the city tournament."

"Thank you, sir, but I want you to give it to the injury player."

He turned red in the face and said, "You mean you don't want it."

"Sir, give it to the injury player and tell him I'm sorry this happen."

He turned, mumbled something, and walked away. I will not put words in his mouth and continue this story, not using the word that is bigger, bigger, bigger than all of us.

On the way back, Mr. Hoover said, "Robert, you know what you did today? You made history. You did something that will never be duplicated in tennis in a hundred lifetimes. You won a tournament with one hit."

"Mr. Hoover, nobody going to believe this. Maybe I should have kept the trophy. People can ask me, the injury player, or Jeffrey. If Jeffrey mom had told him to play, the ambulance would had to turn around and come back."

"This was intimidation at best. You did a good thing, given the trophy away."

"Did he give me the small trophy because I'm a Negro? The *Herald* have a large trophy when the white boys win."

Mr. Hoover laughed and said, "Everybody gets the small trophy. The large one stays in the recreation department in a case. I gave the lady your name, so it should be on the large trophy and the newspaper. Where you get the serve? It was wicked. Your feet came up, and as they were coming down, you made contact with the ball. Robert, this was pure power. The ball was going over hundred miles an hour. He did not have time to react."

"Sir, the workers locked the white people tennis court. I had to use ours, so I took my basketball, knocked over the stuff. Jumped like I am playing basketball and hit an ace on the first try. Jump, serve, the rest is history."

"Robert, I wish things were different."

"Mr. Hoover, Professor Fisher saw me hitting golf balls, putting them in a can a long way. He said, 'Robert, I wish times were different.' Mr. Hoover, thanks for teaching me to play tennis. Honest, I had no interest. I saw the future cheerleaders. I came to get phone numbers."

"Robert, I know. I'm going to tell you something to remember. 'You can catch flies with sugar or honey.'"

"Mr. Hoover, you can also catch flies with stinky stuff. You set us up!" He burst out laughing. (Damn! I recalled Ms. Cleta McLeod making the statement about the early birds and Mr. Hoover calling her back. I thought he scolded her for acting out in front of the boys. In reality, he was using her hotness to get the boys involved in tennis.)

I concentrated on the road. His driving abilities were questionable. I wanted to laugh later, ha-ha.

"Mr. Hoover, you know, in all my short life, it's only one white man who ever thanked me. If Doc was here and told two sports I show natural abilities—golf and tennis—I have no future because of the color of my skin, he would say, 'That's a damn shame!'"

"Robert, on behalf of Doc, 'It's a damn shame!'"

Note: As a Drill Sargent station at Fort Benning, Georgia, I played top-notch tennis with my peers. This story will come later. I invented a charitable tennis game with my peers; however, I do not want the concept stolen like my conception of "park and ride."

Mr. L. W. Hoover
Mathematics & Band

(Mr. Tennis)

Pets: "Papa Luv Beau"(black),
"Beau-Friend" (White)

NOTABLE MENTION

1) I never followed up with the injured player. We were on the same tennis court but in different worlds. Mr. Hoover said, "I am sure his voice returns. Yet Jeffrey, a different story and may need counseling."

2) I went to the Recreation Department numerous times to see my name on the trophy. I will never know; the case was empty and the trophy never displayed again. The racist city manager I'm sure was involved. Unjustified behavior is warranted by the saying, "Damn, white people." Thanks, Mr. Tom Joyner, TJMS Radio.)

3) I searched the sport pages in the *Herald*, looking for my recognition. Nothing! I Folded the paper, and on the back page at my thumb, about the same size, I read, "Robert McLean won this year's city tennis tournament." ("Damn, white people." Thanks Mr. Jay Anthony Brown, TJMS Radio.)

4) Washington (the slave owner) Park's name was later changed for a black man, Mr. W. T. Horton. This was the last city-wide tournament. The white children feared losing their manhood at an early age. "A Legacy is Born."

5) The promise I made to Mr. Charles Marsh senior I have never broken. A three-foot wall with a flat surface—we call it the Hope Wall. It is name not for our wishes as the girls paraded by. The house belonged to Mr. Effren Hope. Mr. Charles Marsh senior was walking by. "Y'all come here! Do you know anybody who do not vote?"

"Yes, sir!"

"Three lousy votes, we could have had our first black alderman. Three lousy votes. Promise me! When you get voting age vote! Hear me!"

"Yes, sir!"

He was too upset to drive and walked away, shaking his head, saying, "Three lousy damn votes."

6) Politics makes me mad. I kept my promise to Mr. Charles Marsh senior. Ups and downs, a big roller-coaster ride. Yet in 2008, my family, voting for the first time, picked a winner. Two years later, all had something to do at midterm. I preached to them about the importance of voting and (staying in my house) what happens when we don't. Living example—people will destroy America from within. They held America hostage like terrorists (say, it's so Joe, VPOTUS).

Prologue: Illness, sickness, disease prevalent in my family scares the hell out of me. Many days I sat with my grandpa as he stirred, became silent, and stirred. I hope (a big) if I'm affected, offspring can read books or listen to audios about my life. I'm sure some trivia in my childhood will make them gasp, such as getting a beat down for drinking white people's water. My historian mother only gave her hardships. Uncle Thomas Hollingsworth stayed far away and died too soon. Grandpa's eyes and skin color information are laid to rest. My daughter Angela Denise, born in "Korea" to dark eyes dark hair people as describe by her then living great grandmother. She said, "The blonde hair and hazel green eyes come from you." (I am black.)

I will end each book by giving recognition to my heroes, two white men who saved my life. Because of God's intervention in the lives of Mr. Squirrel (real name in the later story) and Mr. Jeff Ward, a prominent solicitor, my life flourished and did not end. The life-saving story was told to one person, Mr. Lawrence McLaughlin, my cousin. He would see Mr. Jeff Ward often, and I asked about him. He was fighting the prostrate thing.

"Cousin, Jeff is a great baller who played every play like the game on the line."

Sometimes I would say, "This guy is crazy. We are up by ten points, and he's hustling until the game over." I liked how he would get the ball in the hands of the world's best. Cuz give him a message from me. Tell him "put faith in the one who got the whole world in his hands. The black policemen planned to kill me. I got word later that Mr. Jeff Ward said, "I know Robert. We play ball together, and I'm not going to let him go out like that!" For the first time in my life, I will carry the message with my many siblings. Mr. Squirrel and Mr. Jeff Ward, "You are The Man, until The Man Comes."

God says, *"Let the dead bury the dead."* I am also told old black Mac made the following statement: "I should have taken care of that nigger a long time ago." Well, Captain Mac Dougald, I am telling you what my beautiful mother gave me to live by. Killing me was not in God's plan. God does not make mistakes, and I am *here for a reason*.

Telegraph: Up and coming stories of my life:

School Days	Prayer is powerful
Civil Rights	Park and Ride
Bar boy (not a bully)	Racial Profile (Thanks, Mr. Tom Joyner)
Never Give Up	Nigger's die, over there!
Saddest Day of My Life	Mississippi River Jumpers
Hypocrites Black Revolution	Commanders
Early Army	Not, Rudy
(Ms.) And More!	(Ms.) And More!

United States Army (retired)

In 2001 I promised my son Robert to never cut my
hair until they caught the culprits responsible for
flying planes into the World Trade Center

Closing Prayer, God Bless.

God Bless   Very poor, poor, working poor, homeless veterans, and anyone who needs a place to rest their heads.

God Bless   Families who lost homes and the families on the verge of losing without fault of their own.

God Bless   Culprits unlawful foreclosure on homes after taking bail out money cause these problems. God says, "What go in the mouth is not dirty. What comes out is dirty, it comes from the heart." Dear God, my answer, enough is enough and cannot be used. Dear God, it come from the heart through the mouth of the guilty parties the answer to the question, How much greed is enough?

God Bless   Have, and the Have-mores (2178 plus) who do not pay a fair share of tax rates. Dear God, the greatest day of mankind you walked the earth paid tax. Instructed the collector go down to the river open the fish mouth, and take the talon (money). Oh God, this 1 percent act like they are better than you; however, I differ. Compare, earthly might of these people would not be a pimple on the ass (donkey) you rode.

God Bless   Vice President Joe Biden and family, especially after naming his son Beau, and having the fortitude to shoot people in the face with words, not a shotgun. Terrorist acts in the Hall of Congress are such.

God Bless   President Barack H. Obama and family.

Gob Bless   *Our* United States of America! *Amen.*

Date: 05 April 2012
Status: Proprietary Submission. A complete project.
Represented by: N/A

Dear Publisher,

I am requesting permission to submit my manuscript for evaluation. The working title *Here for a Reason: God don't make mistakes*, is a 205-page, double-spaced, typed manuscript depicting stories of life encounters. This manuscript has not been professionally edited.

Market for this book will be the baby boomers, who carry institution racist baggage. Can reflect on the absolute changing of time and pass on to the younger generation who want to take the country back. Market Patriots who will purchase books in order to rescue homeless veterans.

The book is uniquely better on the market with stories that invaded my life as my memoirs walking with God. The satire portion of the book differ, by walking with the devil. The reader is not only drawn into the stories, but a "Key" is provided to help control emotions, endure, and continue the journey; also, the reader would learn mandate state laws, separation of the races, and denied equal treatment. The book depicts stages of my life, and the stories evolved explain the unjust treatment because of the color of skin. S.A.S.E is enclosed.

I look forward to hear from you,

Sincerely,

Robert Lewis McLean, US Army, Ret.
Post Office Box 1672
Raeford, North Carolina 28376
Date: 05 April 2012

OPENLY DISGRACE

Satirical Styles of Professional Politicians

Robert Lewis McLean, US Army Retired
Post Office Box 1672
Raeford, North Carolina 28376
Phone: 910-583-7928
E: Mail, robertmclean350@gmail.com

Professional Politicians: Born, Live, Die, Messed (Nice Word) Up!

We work for them; some work for big money and self-image. (I do not care if you have jobs, homes, or pursuit of happiness. My sole purpose is to make sure a black man will never be President again.)

Politicos' (Then, Now, Later) stories are for entertainment purpose only! Similarity of people, names, places is coincidental.

Politics and religion make me mad: Laws forbade the mixture of church and state; however, church versus government determines or affects the highest office in the land. Namesake make you uneasy and perceive otherwise a Muslim. Express love for The One you cannot see and not a Christian, a Jew.

There is no controversy in my life with religion. My God gave me an outlet, the Bible. On the other hand, politics is a force to be focused on with grave stipulations on power, wishes, health and welfare of the masses.

Warning to the faint heart: This is *satire!*

THE MAGNIFICENT ONE (THEN)

"Mr. Thousand-dollar Boots, are you busy?"

"Naw, partner, doing what I do best: taking these black jelly beans outah (out) the jar."

"Com-mom in, Henry, I need a honest answer, and I know it's hard to give in our profession, right old boy?"

"Sir, you know the Fifth comes in play before my answer."

"Damn, Henry! Lighten up, boy! I will pardon your German ass, just talk with your native accent. Nobody will understand a damn word you say. All jokes aside, every day I pick these black buggers outah the jar. The next morn they are back. You think the yellow and green beans hooking up making these black babies? Think I should take the yellow beans out?"

"I do not think it will hurt, sir."

"Well, we will see. Enough talk about my troubles. What's on ya mine, partner?"

"Mr. Thousand dollars Boots, I have a proven fact on how we can fix the economy, put money in the party, and line our pockets."

"Well, Henry, you got my attention now. Shoot straight from the lip."

"Sir, Ben Franklin envoy came to European countries seeking help. They have a New World Order and asked for people of character and moral convictions. The envoy pleaded for scholars, scientist, lawyers, doctors, people with job skills, ambitions, and willingness to work. This would be the foundation of the New World Order. Germany, Spain, Italy, and other countries of Scandinavia (white people) made the agreement to send the boats. We will send the people requested.

"The boats arrived and were loaded with people not pleaded for. Mental hospital and prison were empty. Chronically ill, murderers, child molesters, rapists, thieves, con artists (tax collectors, politicians), and people classified the lowest scum on earth.

"The boats returned. Ben Franklin envoy and the welcome to the New World Order were dishearten'. They were misled by the Old Country. Chips are ship in a barrel to minimize damage. Ordinary people have a name for the chips packed in a barrel. Mr. Franklin! Mr. Franklin, it's so many people on the boats, they look like 'Crackers in a barrel!' Sir, the New World Order pleaded with other aristocrats to send them back! 'Take the boats to the Horn of Africa and get free labor.' Mr. Franklin said, 'No, we did not get what we ask for, but God sent us what we need. The foundation will be built on the backs of immigrants. We will ask countries for their tired and poor. We will be known as the "Land of Opportunities." Today we send boats to Africa. Tomorrow people will come on their own accord and do the slave labor. Friends and countrymen, I dread the day our society forget we are all immigrants. Make laws to hindrance concepts we bestowed and forget we all came from other places. Our country will provide, life, liberty, and the pursuit of happiness to all humans, exclude "the blacks." (O my God, this is where The Donald Chump came up with the description inherited from his ancestors the ass-ristocrats (sic).) They are subhuman. To set the degenerates apart from us we will call them "Crackers." Hear ye! Hear ye!'

"Sir, I told you this because the solution to our economy problems are laid out for us. It cost the government 22,000 dollars a year per person housed in the mental institutions. Release them back into society. Look at the money we save for the party and our foreign country friends. You can also buy twenty-two pairs of boots per person."

"Henry, my fellow Americans will not tolerate this! It will be an uproar. There will be rioting in the streets!"

"Sir, you got me! That was good acting!"

"Thanks, Henry. I admit knocking them dead in my filming days."

"Mr. Thousand dollars Boots, American people will never see them. Americans will walk past, run past, drive past them, and sir, we will never have to put security on bridges. The bridges will be manned at all times. This will be their homes."

"Comrade, you Germans are some mean, cold-hearted, ruthless, bastards, but I love ya! Tell me more!"

"Sir, I think we should give them something so they will go away quietly."

"Yeah, Henry. 'If someone fuck me, I want to be kiss first also.' They are saving our economy, conserving our way of life, so give them fifty dollars each."

"Sir, it's far-fetch, too much money. They will not know what to do, and this amount will draw attention."

"You are right, amigo, give them half. Give them twenty dollars."

"Mr. President, sir!"

"Save it, Henry. Cook the books we gave them twenty-five. Give them twenty dollars, and five dollars give to those greedy some bitches, bastards on the hill. Amigo, you personally supervise stuffing the envelopes and deliver at midnight to those leeches. Be careful. The cross-dressing director got eyes and ears everywhere. Hombre, I use to call him cowpoke until I found out his sexual favorite time. I overheard Secret Service talking about a new school in the beltway, and he's a student. Cow-Poke U. is the school name. His favorite subject are bulls, so I call him bull-Poke. Hombre, you know what he says if he want the bull to poke faster?"

"No, sir."

"He says, 'Hee-haw! Heeee-hawww!' Amigo, I learned this shrewdness from my beloved who's doing a damn great job running the country.

"Amigo, if this ever come back to haunt us, we will say money and food were given as countrymen departed the mental institutions. What can we do about the food situation?"

"Sir, a Negro name Carver made this stuff out of peanuts called peanut butter, and the natives love it."

"Did Carver make a lot of money off his invention?"

"Sir, he is paid peanuts!"

"Well, I be damn! Henry, give them twenty dollars, a peanut butter sandwich, and official farewell with my deepest appreciation, giving up medical treatment for the sake of our government."

"Sir, you will go down in history as the 'Magnificent One.' All presidents in the other party will be judge or measure by your success. The party budget plans which take money, dissolve programs from the poor, working poor, middle class, give to themselves and special interest groups will be called 'Marvelous.' Sir, Crackers have a deep-rooted hate for America. We pacified the Crackers telling them no matter the circumstances, the color of your white skin make you better than any black person. Sir, if this office is ever held by a woman or black, the Crackers will unite, gain power, and destroy America from within."

"Hey, partner, that's down the road. It's not our problem. Make a recommendation to the Unofficial President. Put a yes-man in charge of the Treasury so this thing of ours won't blow up in our face. Henry, when you go past the President office, tell my wife she earn every penny of the two million dollars, so knock it off. I will spare you the agony. I let you know the meaning the fifth will not save ya I will have to kill ya ass. My sweetheart, love power and I have a control stick. Tell her to come to The Great Emancipator bedroom. I feel like sleeping on a nigger lover tonight."

"Good night, sir."

"Yeah, boy, nite-nite."

Note: A small segment of *Women Rule the World* (future story): I strongly believe if gender is important. God is a woman and the devil is a man. The highlight of the story is that a woman carried the resolute of the government as her husband battles a sickness; however, she stayed behind the scenes, and the greatness was bestowed on her husband she worshipped and endured. A famous man who happens to be a (historical) president said, "If we had more women in Congress, imagine the things we could accomplish."

I AM ONLY A DJ, BUT (NOW)

"Hey, Mr. Fred."

"Hi ya doing, young blood."

"Mr. Fred, who is that singing in the corridors?"

"He's the king of radio, a giver to society and a great humanitarian. Young blood, you know the house have bugs, so upon arrival you are given a false name. His name is Cisco, and you put a handle on it. We call him Cisco the Klepto. He's a multimillionaire and will take things he feel cannot be bought. Sit down a minute. Put the feather duster down! Since this family move in butlers, maids and Congress have not done a damn thing for three years. Everybody know the little darlings are doing your jobs as chores. Cisco graduated from a black university and one of the very fortune few. Majority of students had to obtain loans from our government. His parents paid cash for his education for sixteen-plus years."

"Mr. Fred, excuse my rudeness. Mr. Cisco was in college all those years, what was his becoming status, a doctor or something?"

"Listen close, son, mumbles are the words. His major is college, minor spades, and elect course chasing tail. Older brother drop a dime. 'Father will make a check call to see how his investment is coming along.' The school did not want to lose cash on hand and would not cheat. School president just happen to mention around people who would cheat proudly his fraternity 'The Q Dogs.' The Qs took over. Chained him to a desk with books galore, microscope, telescope, slide rules, all things educational. The 'Q Dog and Pony show' went off well. Father was satisfied, and the money kept coming for another four years. Cisco was not happy. While placating his father wishes, the band he belong had a gig in the student union. The band blew up, became world famous. A skinny, big-lip kid took his job singing, and he came to the conclusion education stop him from being famous. A tribute to his father, keep kids in school by any means. He has milk crates of albums and started a career as a Disk Jockey. He took all gigs and asked why? He said, 'I only being chain down once.'

"Cisco sidekick is name Poncho."

"Poncho?"

"Wait! Young blood, these famous men have to be shown respect by the young, hear me!"

"Yes, sir. Mr. Poncho is like Mr. Cisco?"

"No, son. They are different as night and day. Poncho is a man of comedy and will do anything for a laugh. He gives back to society when you buy his shigidy (word coined by Mr. Ken Smuckley Mother), hot sauce, suits, shoes, hair salon, nightclub, and such. Old age make you forgettable. Cisco befriend the skinny kid, and they are homey good friends forever. Cisco head got bigger. The ladies say both heads. Voice change and ideally for the radio. Pay dirt ordain 'The King of Radio.'

"Cisco was the first black revolutionary of the airwaves. Racial profiling then, now, later, he would announce the racist cops traps. He is arrested on the air and taken to the police station. He is not book, let go on his own accordance. He thought his radio power endure. Not really. Big brother call the station, pretending father speaking, and the cops release him immediately. Everyone knew father did not play when family involve. His name carry a lot of weight, Mr. Hercules. Cisco said, 'Pop say live by your words, and I gave the cops my word. What I'm going to do Biggem?' 'Well, I'm going to invest in you. I think it's a good thing you doing, voicing your first amendment rights. Take my money, set up shop in New York. Broadcast dealings in Dallas, and when cops come, you are not there. Keep on the move.' 'Thanks, Biggem!' 'Little brother, you have a plane to catch!' 'Biggem, you know I'm going to get the last say so, "Thank God for older brothers like you.""

"The plan worked. One hundred-plus stations—it is all about business. Goals met. Now it was time the king got a queen (not The Queen). We men are in love with Ms. Gladys, a beautiful singer. We knew the lady was out of our league, so we cheered, 'Cisco, go for it.' We wanted the match to happen. I do believe his college-day antics caught up with him, and the classy lady made aware of his college elect subject, chasing tail. Young blood, it's hard for him to shake the college life. Money no obstacle, etch in stone: 'Cannot buy, take it.' These words to live by cause a curse in sporting events. He will pick more losers than winners. Do not ride on his bandwagon. Young blood, the fist curse event to light Cisco sneak into Ms. Glady's room. He took bathrobe, washcloth, and towel. His sidekick, Poncho, said, 'He look in her drawers.'"

"Drawers! Drawers, Mr. Fred!"

"I do not know, son. Poncho got his laughs and moved own. I ponder a long time I wanted to look in Ms. Gladys drawers also. I went to the crime-infested platform to catch the midnight train to Georgia. Change my mind with my life on the line, and the source not reliable. The first curse is bestowed, 'Cisco will never look in these drawers again.'

"Well, son, the next curse deride from Mr. Sweetness, a great football player. Cisco sneak into his room and took his game jersey. Replacement jersey the worst football day of his life. He had a minus 150 yards. He said, 'I'm laying the sport curse down.' Young blood, the third curse is a dosey told to Mr. Robert McLean a famous writer. It came from a man who just happens to be homeless. Cisco came out of this four-star restaurant in Atlanta, picking salad out of his teeth 'cause, he's a vegetarian. Mr. Man, who just happens to be homeless, recognize and call out, 'Cisco! Cisco, baby it's me. I listen to you all the time. Your radio show is like crack I need you every day, so make it worthwhile, baby.' Cisco is a man of integrity, and I believe when he said, 'I gave the homeless man five dollars.' Mr. Man, who just happens to be homeless, told Mr. McLean put a decimal in front with one zero."

"Mr. Fred, he only gave him fifty cents! Mr. Fred, Mr. Cisco is worth millions and gave him fifty cents. He must be one of those damn Republicans!"

"Whoa, Young blood! A famous saying from Poncho: 'Watch out there now!' Son, this is the utmost curse or cuss. Let's not wish this on any law-abiding citizen."

"Sorry, Mr. Fred. Sir, how can Mr. Cisco erase the curses or make his life better and lift this burden?"

"Son, if he would give God the challenge, his problems will be solve. He send donations, and the Bishop do not complain 'cause wealth is plentiful. I think a passage in the Bible scares him. 'It is easy for a rich man to go through the eye of needle than enter heaven.' He went to a beautiful lady of unforseen wisdom, knowledge, and have the gift. Her name is Mrs. Dupre, and she gave him the solution. Quite simply put. 'Give all your fame and fortune to Poncho.'"

"Sir, you think Mr. Poncho will squander his earthly goods?"

"Oh hell, yeah! Without a doubt, and I'm sure as pig pussy is pork! All the fame and fortune, Poncho will join the fraternity who take, never give back, rob the poor give to the rich, a damn Republican.

"One tryst against Poncho I hold dear to my heart. He follow suit and became a vegetarian like us. He went on national television and exposed a hideous fact. Once he became a vegetarian, all he smell is meat. Cisco radio program is head over heels on the wannabes. He hires people from different walks of life. A local man of comedy give an award for exemplified behavior call the 'Bama.' Our home boy is name Huggy. He gave Poncho the Bama of the week for smelling meat."

"Meat? Meat, Mr. Fred?"

"Yeah! Meat! Meat, Young blood."

"Sir, Mr. Cisco and Mr. Poncho have this heavy load, and you told me behind every great man it's a greater woman."

"Son, if a 'true or false' question arises, bet everything, including the kitchen sink, on 'true.' The Articulate One is the most powerful man in the world. However, the Princess is more popular. You have a keen memory, and the beau (beautiful) name is Ms. Gena. She is complex, highly educated, and use these big-ass words to tell you how stupid you are. We wanted her to marry Mr. Gerald, a famous singer, but he confused the hell out of us. We decided to leave it to nature. Ms. Gena is complex, and he said, 'What a simple man like me to do.' Mr. Gerald came back later saying, 'You got that I wanna slap your mama kind of love.' I decided not text or call the radio show. Let love endure. Opposites attracts. The men came to the conclusion, personality, conduct, and emotions will be judge by the 'key' to a famous writer memoirs, Mr. Robert McLean, *Here for a Reason*. Events in life make you happy, glad, or sad, continue on the journey. Event of life make you mad, *change* only after researching facts! The day Ms. Gena became outrageous mad, a doctor called the radio show."

"What's his name Mr. Fred?"

"His name is Dr. George Wallace."

"What is his expertise?"

"Son, he is a man of comedy and a butt doctor."

"Proctologist, Mr. Fred?"

"Naw, son, he tell you a joke, you or your mama usually be on the ass end! The beautiful lady did not take kindly to the behind jokes and got super mad. She forgot the only rule of the radio show. The one and only Queen of Soul is shown unduly respect, everyone else is fair game. The rule was not adhere by the beautiful lady, so changes have to be made. Cisco said, 'Dr. Wallace played by the rule of the radio show. The rule is the only person gets respect is the Queen of Soul. She demands a little bit. Ms. Gena went outside the box, so the first thing we need to change is her name.' Only after researching the facts because she got mad. The many mood swings a name to coexist will be Sybil. All in favor say, 'Da roof, da roof, da roof on fire!' Cisco said, "Old Gena is no more! Miss Sybil is the new prima donna of radio!" With the new name, she became comfortable in her skin and vowed 'get back.' She is the baby sister, and her feelings should come before Dr. George Wallace. First get back, expose to the world, Poncho was a vegetarian, a cool three minutes. She did an old-school trick. She pretended leaving by loudly closing the door. She waited in the closet, observing Poncho area of operations. Poncho sneaked back, look around, and retrieved a greasy brown bag from his bottom desk drawer. Prior to Poncho going on television in ten minutes, she witness him divulge a whole chicken, meat and bones, in five minutes. She knew the real deal when he said on the television program, 'After becoming a vegetarian, all I smell is meat.' She laughed like no tomorrow because she knew Poncho is smelling his breath while talking. He is not lying. 'Get back' for Cisco is short and to the point, because he signs the payroll checks. She will not endorse his books. His two-car garage is stacked with books. He stay on a golf course and have to park the family cars on the fifth fairway behind the house."

"Mr. Fred, is Mr. Poncho a lost cause? Everyone matchmaking except him."

"Well, you like what you like, and Poncho like white meat. We hope for the beautiful Ms. Natalie, a singer. She is half white, but Poncho said, 'Let it be.' I ran it by her, and she responded, 'I am looking for love. However, Poncho in my life, I will be catching hell.'"

"Mr. Poncho sound like a person of fun. Why he does not come to the Big House?"

"Protection is the reasoning. The only rule of the Big House, no cursing, and Poncho is well-verse in the art. You know, the young man people say are from the West Indies. He is from the south side of DC. He came with an attitude and pants sagging to his knees. He thought he has clout here because a relative is mayor for life and known for snorting up all the snow. The Enforcer of the Big House rule stalked him, waiting on a chance to pounce. A matter of hours, he said, 'Hell, I'm not gonna do that. It's not on my resume.' The Enforcer of the Big House rule toed him up and slapped the taste out of his mouth. Sobering loudly, 'I only said hell and hell in the Bible.' She said, 'Son I'm telling you something and don't forget it. Hell is in the Big House also.' He's now around here talking proper."

"New-York-City proper, Mr. Fred?

"Naw, across-the-big-pond proper. He ask me, 'Tea, oh chap?' I jump back and pull my razor. Now he's walking around with belt and suspenders. She literally scared the hell out of him. Yeah, she toed him up and wash his mouth out with lye soap. Cisco is sheltering Poncho for his sake. Have you ever heard a person talking old country English funny?"

"Not in my short lifetime, Mr. Fred."

"Well, in 1970, the first black man of comedy was a football player in Britain named Mr. Charles A. Williams. I will cut the story short and go into detail the next time. His presentation was called 'Ye Old Flower.' He copy his antics after a famous man of comedy who scares the living hell out of white people, Mr. Paul Mooney. He kept white people in a Pandora's box. He is world famous for the Romney act *Flip or Flop.* 'White people, you don't be quiet. I will move next door to you. White people, you don't laugh. I will move next door to you. White people sneaking out. Get your tails back and sat down, or I will move next door to you.'"

"Mr. Fred, where you get your source of information?"

"Son, I use too say, 'I tell you, I'll have to kill you.' No more, we have to enlighten our younger generations by word of mouth. The key is the radio. This came from *The Tom Joyner Morning Show, Little Known Black History Facts.*"

"Sir you have time to tell me how the Big House Enforcer got her name 'Miss Sweet Honey Ray, She does not play.'"

"Son, since this family move in, all we have time. The families before were nasty and thought we were really slaves. This family got it going on, treat us with respect, and I love how they pick up after themselves. We are bless, and I strongly pray for another four years. Miss Sweet Honey Ray She does not play and Poncho have something in common. They are from the racist state of South Carolina. Poncho, the capital Columbia and she from the paper mill town, Georgetown. The family reunion conducted down south, everyone came back to the roots of the family. The boxing Champion of the World showed up with three white ladies. This is not odd. 'The Smith Family' was there. He called out, 'Hi ya, Auntie, still got those superfast hands?' The showboating made him get slap five times before he realized it. 'Oo-wei, Auntie, those fists are sweet as honey. I'm second nature to you. I want to give you the name Sugar Ray.' She said, 'Naw, Sugar, you are the World Champion and had the name first. I like when you said my fist are sweet as honey so I will shout from the highest mountain, "I am Miss Sweet Honey Ray, and I don't play." Sugar, you are going to get a good down home whup ass for bringing those white ladies.' 'I know,

Auntie, and I promise they will step as soon as possible.' 'Sugar, you are the World Champion, and you know that don't mean ditty squat down here. These good old boys with badges, guns, and judges, our fists do not match up. (A legacy is born, and the boxing genes inherited by the Princess. On television, the Princess knocked Mr. Al Roker, the weatherman, out of the picture.) Sugar, get rid of the white ladies and live to fight another day.' 'Auntie, I'm praying for a way to get these ladies away from me.' Prayer works, another family member walks up crying. He has on a thousand-dollar tuxedo shirt mess up with colors and wetness. His face was distorted and not easy recognizable. Miss Sweet Honey Ray She does not play said, 'Smoke? Is that you, Smoke?' 'Hi'ya doing y'all.' 'Why are you crying? Happy to be here or the mess up shirt? What the deal baby?' says Sugar. 'The shirt not important, got plenty just being told Mr. Simon, the white clown, is my dad. I confronted him, and the stuff on my shirt are tears of a clown. Auntie, Sugar, I am leaving before other family secrets are revealed. I'm getting while the getting is good. I want to be a distance lover.' 'Smoke, I'm going to fix you a plate to go and Sugar need to talk to you while I'm gone.' Sugar told Smoke, 'I need a favor. Auntie made me realize I'm too dark to have these white ladies down here. Smoke, you can play the part with the hair, complexion, and eyes. Would you take the ladies off my hands?' 'Where are they going?' 'Smoke, Chicago, New York, or anywhere that thang between their legs tak'em. Here's money for the bus tickets.' 'Keep your money, Sugar. What are family for? What is the name of these fine-ass mamas?' 'Smoke, I could not tell you the names if my life depend on it. I call the blonde anytime, brunette most of the time, and the redhead all the time.' Smoke said, 'Sugar, when you see me again, call me Father time.' Miss Sweet Honey Ray She does not play gave the travelers a half hog with fixing, and they left in peace. Son, since Sugar shuck the good-time white ladies, the extra room was filled with down-home goodies. He has enough to start an eatery in Chicago, call 'Sugar Ray's Shucks.' She gave him the family secret. Buy your meat in Kansas City and play the sides. If you are buying in Missouri, say, 'The last time you bought the meat in Kansas, great results, vice versa.' The biggest part of the secret:

do not buy the meat down south. The locals are too attach, sleep, alleged sex, ride hogs in pickup trucks, wrestle, and treat as family members. This is inhumane, and the meat taste bad.

"Young blood, can you see what Cisco is doing?"

"Yes, sir. He stop in front of the W plaque and looking around."

"Well, I hope he take that damn thang. It's ten warehouses full. He could not give them away. He gave some to the homeless. Plaques beat him back arrive COD with a message, 'We are homeless, not stupid.' The only person who did not return was the man who shot his friend in the face and demanded an apology for getting in his line of fire."

"Mr. Fred, he took it down, looked around, and wipe his ass with it. Maybe that's what the W mean. He put it back and spit on it. He must really hate W."

"A lot of people do, son, a lot of people do. I know he's important. He just barge in the Articulate One office and did not need a letter like the governor requesting an appointment. Barbershop said, 'The wrong lady was shot.' Son, it is not in God plan. God do not make mistakes. She is *Here for a Reason* Young blood, I think she saw the light. The crazy Republicans put forth a bill to carry loaded firearms in public domain, police stations, courtrooms, and the most heated, racist, bigot place on earth—her bedroom. The first time in state history she veto her crazy Republican Party ideas. Son, God works in mysterious ways, and thank God, the Articulate One ooze class. Angry black man like me would had bury the finger up her racist ass."

"Checking out, Mr. Fred. Thanks for everything."

"Son, same time, same place tomorrow I will tell you about the black souls who built this shigidy (word coined by Mr. Ken Smuckley

Mother). You know why the front entrance door is inside and open inside?"

"No, sir!"

"The Big House is Christian. No black person will ever walk through the front door. The slaves could not go through and had to walk around, so they hung the door to accommodate. The darkest slave name Mr. Nicodemus was single out, beat to death with a bull whip on the Big House lawn as a demonstration and reminder if caught or told a black violated the front door sacred rule. The real reason his face was like a black pearl and smooth as a baby behind. White ladies would make a scene rubbing his face. White men noticed, and the light-skinned house slaves resented the attention given. White men came to the conclusion the ladies were sharing a secret. When they rub his face, a big bulge appears in his pants. He haunted people nightly. They escaped and went to Kansas. I hear you thinking, Young blood, why he haunted his own people? Back then, the house slaves were siblings of the white masters. They did not like a beautiful black pearl in their mist. A plan is made to get rid of him. Upcoming celebration, all slaves were brought in for entertainment. The field slave with comic prowess was name Jay. He poked fun of his existing and the establishment with a segment call, 'Is this chain own.' Son, the vice president used the 'chain own' term, and the Republicans went ape-shit crazy. They want to keep the 'chain own' invisible around Americans' neck. Sorry, I got sidetracked, back to the story. A high yellow lady befriended Jay, the field slave, and told how he could knock the white folks dead with laughter at the celebration. She promise if he carry out her plan, she will also sleep with him. The plan, while Mr. Nicodemus slept, put coal dust on his neck and face. The highlight of the party bring on Mr. Nicodemus and the senator wife from the racist state of South Carolina will do the honor. The white ladies waited with anticipation of witnessing the big bulge. She put on a white glove and rub his face. Looking at the blackness on the glove, she fainted. She went into depression. Bad health endure, so Washington, the slave owner, offered the senator any two slaves of his chose. He took a pecan tan woman (bear his children) and Jay, the field slave."

"Mr. Fred, Mr. Poncho is from South Carolina and love white women. You think they are relatives? They have the same attributes with white women and clowning."

"I am calling Professor Gates and checking this out. Let you know next week. The runaway slaves showed remorse and were sorry. The joke cost the life of an innocent man. White people gave them land in dry gulch, a barren place own by Native Americans. Both people were downtrodden, so they became beautiful friends. Mr. Nicodemus came in dreams, shouting, 'Fix it! Make it right by me!' The people came to the conclusion, name the town after him. He will be satisfied. The town they formed is called Nicodemus Kansas. This did not work. The onslaught continue with vengeance. The town is on the Reservation. A meeting took place, and a suggestion to apply for a grant and aid to build a resort and casino complex. The resort and casino complex is named in remembrance of Mr. Nicodemus, and the haunting stopped. To this day it's called, Lodgepole.

"Washington, the slave owner, sent an envoy with a message. 'Please come back. I miss my children.' They sent back a reply, 'We are ex-slaves. We are not stupid!' Out of fear he may come after them, they made a fake town. This is the idea use in the Mel Brooks cowboy film. They broke up. The light-skin went to South Dakota. The dark-skin went to Nebraska. (Today the towns still stand and both named Lodgepole.)

"You might notice the little darlings running in and out. That's my doing. They like to see me laugh at history. I will also tell you which one of the little darlings carry the kick-ass boxing gene."

"Sir, I think I know. The Articulate One always hold her hand because she will give you the look, yes the look: 'I'm Little Miss Sweet Honey Ray, and I don't play.' C-ya, Mr. Fred."

"Not if I c-ya first. C-ya, Young blood."

Cisco went into the office of the Articulate One. He greeted him with "My Big Chief" (only person authorize to use this greetings; because, of equal treatment under the law a lady had the opportunity. After seeing the Articulate One wife Princess beat up Mr. Al Roker. A safety net is installed to save her life. she is denied greeting the Articulate One as My Big Chief. We call this lady "Mama Bees." Stand for beautiful, bodacious, black billionaire, and I will only give her initial as respect must be shown. Her initial is "Oprah." I mean Oh, Oh, Oh, it's *The Tom Joyner Morning Show*.) My man Cisco staying out of trouble? Sir, it's easy when you leave Poncho behind until he finish counseling. Cisco make him come correct. Mom (only person, everyone else including Mr. Jenkins must call her Miss Sweet Honey Ray She does not play) will toe him up and wash out his mouth with lye soap. My man, how is the wife? I got people tracking the information before I send congratulations. The story goes Mrs. Fitness climbed up and down Mount Killer Man mountain in nine inches spike heels backward. Cisco, you married a superwoman! My sources identify the culprit, and signs point toward your sidekick, Poncho. My Big Chief, maybe some truth to this. He was tasked to gather her equipment for the climb. He probably did this in order to get laughs. He's a joker and will do anything to fulfill. I will tell you, man, from the highest office in the land, "Poncho is the king of comedy."

"Sir, working on something secret?"

"I'm just a DJ, but like Mr. Kevin Hart, a man of comedy. I know a lot of shigidy (word coined by Mr. Ken Smuckley Mother). Well, I'm working on the State of the Union. Got any ideas?"

"Easy! Sir, a proven fact if you want people to hear you instead of listening, tell them a minimum of three times. This is your third time. Do not change a damn thing. I'm only a DJ, but this is logic."

"Thanks, man, you made my day. Six figures people working on this, and you just nail it!"

"A DJ, but I know money cannot be solicited from you in this office, so I will make a shot out to the homeless shelter for veterans or anyone who need a place to rest their heads. Donations are warranted, sir! While I got your ears."

"Cisco, I heard the presidential ear jokes on the program."

"Sorry, sir! If I am a betting man, I would say not so!" You are right my big ears I mean My Big Chief, Ha-Ha. Sir, the newest up rise are homeless female veterans, and it's a damn shame. A double-edge sword, fight our wars, then out of uniform have to fight Republican legislatures. "War On Women!" Sir Virginia Governor *ultra sound* believes the economy can be save by looking in vaginas for oil. The ploy patient pay for the procedure and the money go to the Republican Party. Cisco struggles are on to fight the absurd lawmakers who are taking women's rights back to the 1950s.

"Sir, a real-life jerk gave me an idea on your plan to in-source jobs. Huggy, a program family member, gave him the name Sperm man. He is an activist for the trailer park tea party Republicans trash white pussy, I mean white people. He's a common brother with Poncho. They love white meat. He's married, so that give him a third eye on the little head that have more brains than the one on his shoulders. He made me hot by saying, 'You are poor because you want to be.' I said, 'Nigger, please!' I do agree when he says, 'Your in-source jobs on American shores do not go far enough.' Sir, did you know jobs are coming back, but they are bringing the cheap labor force with them.

"We are land of the plentiful. Sir, you cannot give away stuff like the good old days without stipulations. A man who just happens to be homeless, a disagreement evolve. I tried to settle our differences by offering a peace gesture. I took fifty Jay Anthony Brown suits on Old Wilmington Road with fifty pairs matching alligator shoes. If I had to do over, I would take the items to the Salvation Army boxes. Mr. Man, who just happen to be homeless, made me feel lower than whale poop. I approached the bridge. Mr. Man recognize and call out, 'Cisco baby, I am hooked on your show. It's like crack, got to have it daily. Make it worth my while, baby.' Sir, people from all walk of life white, black, Asian, Latino, women, and children came from under the bridge and a trash dumpster. I marvel how it's hoist up and level. I found out later Mr. Man was an army veteran fellow officer in the Army Corp of Engineers. I told Mr. Man I got fifty suits for you all, and he said, 'Cisco baby, are the suits dry clean?' 'No.' 'Well, bring them back with receipts. We might take them. We are just homeless, not stupid.' 'Mr. Man, I got fifty pairs of alligator shoes for you all'. He replied, 'Are the shoes shine?' 'No.' 'Well, shine the shoes. We might take them. We just homeless, not stupid.' I lost my composure and shouted, 'Negro, please, these shoes are expensive and self-shine!' The cool voice with the captive audience, he said, 'Cisco, do not be so mean. Use cotton balls and Vaseline. We just homeless, not stupid.' I went home dejected, rushing to get in the arms of my superwoman. I needed a hug and bad. She console me and laid it on the line. 'Luxury item in poverty is not justified. The people are just homeless, not stupid.' I told you this because we have luxuries we cannot afford and not beneficial. Companies stand with American or sale the items to the people, making your products away from our shores.

"Sperm man is a businessman and knows the crooked end of capitalism. I came to the conclusion Americans have to be compensated after being abuse by members of the fat Kats, Kittens Klan of Congress, and corporations pursuing greed. Jobs for which Americans are paid thirty thousand a year went away where people are paid fifty cent a day. Yet the goods are bought back duty free or low tariff. Sir, if the Republicans gain power, a plan concocted will go in effect. The name is Territory Tax (pay tax in the countries which house your outsourced business). Bring the money to our shores tax-free for safekeeping. *Remember Cuba Revolution!* 'Why in the hell Americans are fleeced!' Pay a 500 percent tax. This is song percentage after your debut at the Apollo Theater in New York City. Make it right by America or let your company host country safeguard your money and sale your products to the people making fifty cents a day. Don't get me wrong, sir, companies have the right to leave and fat Kats, Kittens Klan of Congress will not block them. However, previous employees have to be satisfied before goods are brought back to our shores. A number plan derived from Sperm man. The plan is 'ten, ten, ten, ten.' Ten years' taxable salaries, ten years' health and dental, ten years' education, trade school, and ten years' usage of the Chevrolet Volt (by which a fat bigot racist radio journalist got it wrong on American abilities to create), option to buy for five hundred dollars. Sir, this is song percentage after your debut at the Apollo Theater in New York City."

"Cisco, thanks for the enlightenment, and I promise the issues will be taken serious. My man, seal lips are the key. I do not want the old mother muckers on Capitol Hill to get wind of this and muck it up. Anything else from a DJ, but point of view?"

"Yes, sir! The Congressional Fleet should be all electric cars. Sir, the fat Kats, Kittens Klan of Congress poked fun about the Chevrolet Volt after giving tax credits to big oil companies. The fat Kats, Kittens Klan of Congress desires to ride in Mercedes, the means should not be provided by American taxpayers but the organizations they work for (big oil, big banks, Crotch Brothers, ALEC, other culprits). Sir, you sang, 'Mr. Green, we have to go Green,' so 'Let's Stay Together.' Sir, I am out of here. My body here with you, but my mind is at home."

"My man, Cisco, later man."

"My Big Chief, God bless you and your family. God bless America!"

"Hear you, man, for real, no joke about the ears. Luv ya, man!"

"My Big Chief, I have to be me and must make you aware. You shot me a line that rhyme with hear, real, and the big presidential ears, so I'm leaving with got your back!"

"Okay, my man, my man.

Note: Uniqueness in our lives is the true friend. Hold back no punches; tell you like it is. Surround sound is pleasing. The admirers telling you how great you are spare or stretch the situations to alleviate just challenges or confrontations. Admiration is the "Titanic" of politics; when there is a downfall, people will tell you untruths to keep the conception: All Things Are Going Great!

POLITICS, AN UGLY BUSINESS (LATER)

Turncoats are people whose actions are not conducive with the past, present, or future surroundings. Actions are not determined by race, color, creed, nature origin, sexual orientations, or religion. Amazingly, another word coexists with the same venom; it is called "nigger." Main job or purpose of a true turncoat/nigger is to go against the grain with outlandish solutions to America's problems. Mentally, exhibitions put in context the destruction of our country, "Our way or the highway." (Thanks, MSNBC's Mr. Ed Shultz.) Ironic, outlandish solution examples: Stand Your Ground Law, which is a license to kill an innocent child armed with a bag of candy and iced tea. This law should also kill the chances of another Bush's bull's eye on the presidency and destroying our way of life. The Weeper of the House is dead set the 1 percent the so-called rich are job creators. He looked foolish when he walked away and returned to the podium and said, "Where the jobs!" He knows the answer; the job creators are creating! Another outlandish solution is voter suppression. Where is the fraud! Where are the basic concerns attacking something of lesser means? The outlandish solutions tried through trickery cause greater problems.

Our American way of life is treated as a commodity, and the powerful voters, women, are treated as an "interest group." We are pimp slap daily by the turncoat/nigger, and this is unpatriotic. A commodity side of the equation is demonstrated by the turncoat/nigger, rising gas prices and never lowing gas prices due to speculations. My fellow Americans are not stupid. We know this is a political ploy to unseat the president of the United States. We know it looks like shit, smells like shit; turncoats/niggers do not have to keep rubbing in our faces. We get the message. "Speculation of gas prices is *shit!*" I cannot erase the memories of the shit-eating grins on the faces of the turncoats/niggers testifying before Congress. The overconfident behavior expressed, "We got you, and nothing you can do about it." It was laughable. Some members of Congress are owned lock, stock, and barrels of *oil* by them. They are protected.

This is a satire; a small group can afford to laugh, the reminder cry. My fellow Americans, a motto to be grasped is "Hope, you must vote." The turncoat/nigger laughs first; Americans will laugh last. We will come together, vote, and turn those smiles upside down.

Our past we cannot change; however, tidbits of the past and present will give you tools to prejudge the future. A famous turncoat/nigger orchestrated the worst presidential run in American history. The rule to live by in politics: make your weakness the opponents. This venom is prevalent today. This bastard said, "I regret I only have many lies to give to my country."

A short journey back in time starts with a turncoat's/nigger's use of the prescribed system. The turncoat/nigger will turn the tide. On national television, in front of the world, the turncoat/nigger called the leader of the world a *lie*. He made the decisive vote in favor of sending the great racist state of South Carolina jobs to Central America. The reason he gave is "South Carolina should be torn down so Central America can be build up in our racist images. There was no mention of the car-trunk-load of money distributed among his political party and Republican judges. Politics is an ugly business! In a no rights-to-work state, the turncoat/nigger went all out to get this giant airplane company. The half-brained people of South Carolina have been sold down the river without a paddle again. South Carolina is a stopover as the rights on the giant airplane company are already in the hands of Central America. A trainload of money was paid in advance and hid in containers with war goods. The BDO computers went down, and the money shipped to the war zone. The turncoat/nigger is pleading for extending the wars; as long as boots are on the ground, there's a good chance the money can be directed to the Cayman Island, Swiss Swede banks, or brought back. Mr. Ed Shultz MSNBC, in *The Ed Show*, talks about the miles of empty containers brought to our shores, and we do not have goods to return. The president speaking in Miami, Florida, was surrounded by empty containers. After the speech, he went immediately to Central America and pleaded American interests case. The president's plan is called "principles of the revolving door."

"People of the Summit of the Americas. The fat Kats, Kitten Klan of Congress sold you American jobs. Your lives have improved greatly. I'm speaking on behalf of the American people, not the fat Kats, Kittens Klan of Congress. They scratched your back. Now I need you to scratch the back of the American taxpayer and buy goods made in America."

The turncoat/nigger will get his fat Kats, Kitten Klan colleagues to make laws to bring the containers back from the war zone. This may be the first bi-partisan agreement in three and a half years. The remainder car-trunk-load of money will be given to organizations to influence or buy the presidential elections. A turncoat/nigger in the highest office like Vietnam Airplanes was sent to bring French gold back to America. The containers will bring the money back to the Professional Politician Party.

Note: The later story of turncoat/nigger of America will not play out; ending will be suspect and the discretion of the outcome to you the Reader. This is a satire; names, places are coincidental. A senator broke the camel's back as he is prejudged by his namesake. In pursuit of the highest office in the land he said, "This is not white America, this is not black America, this is not Asian America, this is not Latino America, this is the United States of America! God bless America!"

LAUGH TO KEEP FROM CRYING
(FOREVER MORE)

Politics is not a religion as implied by a mega church pastor in Dallas, Texas. It's like the Mormon Church, a cult. A man running for the highest office carries this baggage. The pastor preaches the latter and will interpret choices for his church members. Out of his mouth he will endorse the devil because the incumbent is a Christian. He will not support his Christian brother because he just happens to be black. Laugh, to keep from crying.

The leaders of the churches have great power over the flocks. A majority of the church members strive to please, work, and stay in good faith with the man. Members shun the pew pit blasting and this practice is call "head hunting." A voting occurrence happens when a church bus with many beautiful ladies, drove up. Inside, eight ladies were staring at me. "My God, I better do a quick check, maybe a bugger on my nose." Finally a sweet beautiful lady spoke up. She said, "Excuse me, mister, I'm a Democrat, but I need to vote for Bush." The tall, skinny black man said, "We cannot split the vote." He said, "We are Democrats. We have to vote Democrat."

I set the record straight. "Ma'am, it's okay to check the Bush block and remain Democrat." She gave a sigh of relief, and the ladies followed suit. I whispered to her, "Why are you splitting your vote?"

"The reverend told us to do this, and he personal told each one of us who to watch, make sure everybody do what he says."

Wow! This was intimidation at best; by the way, the administration gave large sums of money to churches for human services with no strings attached. President Bush (W) won the great state of North Carolina. Laugh to keep from crying.

In 2008, early voting a line of 150-plus people, mostly blacks, were pinching noses and moving out of line. A white man with bad body odors caused the malady. Army veteran, who smelled death; I got behind him as we moved hurriedly to the front. The old lady checking names said, "Ray, I haven't seen you in years. How have you been these days?"

Mr. Ray said, "It's being sixteen years, but I know this one is important, and I feel I have to vote." He cast his vote for Senator John McCain, only without sitting, and gave his ballot to the recorder. I love my America and curse the Professional Politicians voting trickery to suppress the vote. A man whose clothes were rags, was unclean, and needed personal hygiene expressed his civic duty granted by the Constitution. Laugh to keep from crying.

Politics has provided an array of comedy. The lady with the man-face, running for president, voted for health care for her family. Thirty minutes later, standing on the steps of Congress, she barked, "The first thing we need to do is repeal Obamacare!" Ms. Politic Gab is wrong as usual. How much money can be saved if the Fat Kats, Kittens Klan of Congress paid own insurance? Ms. Politic Gab always displays outrageous behavior. The audacity to call the president of the United States a tar baby. The political scheme gives weakness attributes to others into play. Ms. Politic Gab calls his name often and secretly desires to have his offspring.

Satire in politics can be misleading and taken seriously. A satirist created a great story on immigration, called Self-Deportation. If America's economy is suffering, laws are not conducive with equal treatment under humanity standards, people will go back to native countries. A new category of people will be depicted called third-class citizens. The *verbal* plan by the Florida Latino lawmaker is a smoke screen to cash in on the vote. I differ when people say his amendment to the Green Act will create second-class people. This class has been in place over two hundred years, Negroes. Self-Deportation is a joke taken seriously by the Republican nominee for president; however, Mr. Etch-a-Sketch may have a leg to stand on and convince people that American jobs are not in America; look behind you. American jobs are in your native country! Laugh to keep from crying.

The most hilarious script in the history of satire in politics goes to the late great man of comedy, Mr. Richard Pryor as the First Black President. The script touches on extreme agendas in the past, by which, the real first black president faces the same obstacles today. Unemployment will determine the outcome of the presidential elections. Mr. Chris Matthews's (*Hardball* on MSNBC) ideology on the subject: 8 percent, the incumbent wins; 9 percent, Mr. Etch-a-Sketch wins. A tidbit in the script gets black unemployment down to 10 percent. White America unemployment will be erased. White unemployment will not exist. The logic is crude, but true.

The rally cry: we want smaller government! Government will influence our way of life! Oh Lord, disaster comes a calling, and the response is deafening. Watermelon tears flowing, the lady standing in the remnants of a mansion in the great country of Texas shouted in the camera, "Where is the president of America! Our President Perry being here where is he!" Not a laughing matter, it appears ironic that states exploring hate, bigotry, racism, and other malice toward humankind are struck, torn down to be rebuilt. A preacher from the great state of Alabama on national television said, "We are not being punished. People say this about us because we are still fighting the War Between the States. Confederates Heritage by any means. We will starve before lowering the rebel flag. This is just a natural act." The conclusion, the Alabama preacher and believers' card to conduct church functions shall be revoked. A natural act is God.

How naive people cannot see the light? A review of a natural act displayed like a dart game. The dart hit a bull's eye a town in Governor Vaginal Ultrasound state of Virginia. Governor Vaginal Ultrasound badmouths the president on every issue and policy. The town is the most racist in the Union. People of color do not reside there because of maltreatment. The Republican Congress stole the postal service kitty of fifty billion dollars. The postal service was discontinued; a lifelong resident went to South Florida to retrieve Confederate flags. He had an extended stay of two additional weeks. His order and the items had to be made. When he returned with a sun tan, the people treated him differently. His wife of twenty-five years went running down the street, shouting, "A nigger in my house!" She brought the police back with a warning, "You do not want to be a victim of this thing of ours, stay in the house!" The police position cars as you enter or exit the town; their sole purpose is vigorous racial profiling. The racist town was hit with the elements of Earth, Wind, Fire (not the greatest band in the land), wrath from God. One town singled out as Sodomy. Governor Vaginal Ultrasound with the shit-eating grin on his face offered an invitation to the president to come witness the destruction firsthand. He will eat crow and accept federal aid for the sake of the town on his terms. Governor Vaginal Ultrasound did not man-up or do a face-off with the president. He could have walked to the White House, but he wanted to play politics and maintain the superiority outlook determined by the color of his skin. He is one of many who think they are better than the president because of this perception. The invite was sent by playing the media. The president gave his response to the media also, "Tell Governor Vaginal Ultrasound, I'm damn busy!" Laugh to keep from crying.

Note: I met a man in Memphis, Tennessee. We were as different as night and day. We voiced our opinions steadily. After two hours of debating, we could or would agree on one thing only. All the many problems we have, we are the greatest nation on earth. God bless America!

Date: August 28, 2012
Status: Propriety Submission. A complete project
Represented by: N/A

Dear Publisher,

I am requesting permission to submit my manuscript for your evaluation. The working title "Openly Disgrace, Satire of Professional Politicians/ Mere Men of Religion Influences," is a 50-page double-space manuscript depicting humorous short stories on generic issues, concepts, as a rule of thumb to cherish laughing to keep from crying.

This manuscript is being professional edited and will be ready for publication.

The target market for this book is people classified in politics as liberal, progressive, independent, sever conservative, conservative, as opposite ideology open season to ridicule with blessing. My short stories reflect on the absolute changing of times, by which, exemplified past, present, future endeavors downplaying a humorous side to problems faced or pushed down our throats as the gossip truth.

The book is uniquely best for the target market as prescribed. Laughter at the opposite classification in politics is healing. Laugh to keep from crying at people perceived to be more ignorant on issues affecting our way of life. The political market is scripted and favors 1 percent of the population who is mega wealthy. The bold part of this agenda is money is power and is pursued or gathered at the expense of others. A victim of this travesty, to soothe aches and pain, laugh.

The book is educational, exposing a different outlook in politics and highlights humor in laws. The epitome of the world, nations mock our systems and laugh at our shortcomings. We do not practice what we preach and make excuses, by which, not holding merit are hilarious. Attributes to support this ideology:

1) A stoic writer, Mark Twain's outlook on description of the United States Congress: "They are idiots, criminals, and dumb as fleas."
2) Republican Governor's solution to birth control: woman go own an aspirin regiment, put it between your knees, and keep it there.
3) Republican Governor War on Women signs into law a procedure invading a vagina without permission. While she is State Mandate Rape, his solution is "Close your eyes."

Generally speaking, the world frowns on the above categories; however, due to human ignorance and no remorse for others, a green light to ridicule is warranted. This is satire!

I look forward to hearing from you,

Sincerely,

Robert Lewis McLean, US Army, Retired
P.O. Box 1672
Raeford North Carolina 28376
Phone: 910-587-4438 aristobookings@gmail.com

RED BEARD AND THE BLACK TIE
(ETERNALLY FEAR MONGERING)

A beating down physically or mentally by the prescribed law and order is a national travesty. Physical abuse suffer not by Mr. Rodney King (can't we just get along), the aftermath of death and destruction which follow. The guilty parties walk free. Mentally Abuse widespread a teenager walking home, Mr. Trayvon Martin, armed with a bag of candy and iced tea was killed by George (9 mm) Zimmerman, by which, signs of the times are coming into play and he will walk free. The groundwork is in place to get rid of the lady judge. Put a minimal price on the death of a black person, 150,000 dollars. The judge reasoned that George (9 mm) Zimmerman had a meager income. Reverse the role of the players—*bail denied*. The bleeding hearts contributed, reported 200,000 dollars on his web site. The judge was tricked, maybe or not. He refused to raise the price of killing a black person in this society. Mr. Trayvon Martin added to the list of black people deprived even in death the solitude of having live in a human just America.

Fear brings out the worst of us as determined by a secret society in American. The light was turned on by the secret society on the day a black man was sworn in as president of the United States. Treason is prevalent. Motto of the secret society: "The man, not his plans." We will make him the worst president ever and make people aware a black cannot hold the highest office in the land. We will not support him on any policies, even the ones we produced. The standard we live for eight years, we know how to do this, so let's put it into play. We know in our hearts the word we want to use to call and dehumanize him. We will use the code name "Black Guy." Since I'm not in government and was kicked out as speaker of the house, charges of treason cannot be adhere. The Tan man who was chicken shit thinking this not a good idea will pay. The bastard could not see past two years. This thing of ours is for four years, and since Mr. Words Without Knowledge put this together, I'll run for president and want the full support from the secret society. We will go against the norm, attacking women, students, poverty, jobs and set in play the "obstructionist plan." Our motto will come from the wife of the great one who says, "Just say no." Prove our case and point we are at a steak house less than a mile from the Black Guy show. The menu of the secret meal consists of fried chicken, ham hocks, collard greens, black-eyed peas, corn, cornbread, and desert watermelon. After consuming four plates, Newt decided to send the tab to the RNC chairman, the colored man. He told the gathering, "I'm adding a little something, something to the tab for the people back home who prepared this great meal." The men were scared to resist because in Newt's own words, "He is a two-headed snake." A problem came when the steak house manager requested cash for the box of steaks to be sent to Georgia. He knew the morals of the people. They could not be trusted; they were Republicans. Newt said, "I forgot my wallet. Eric, Paul, be good ole boys and take care of this little matter." Paul whispered to Eric, "I bet that cracker barrel bastard going to sell the steaks to pay for his trip up here." (More information on the secret society is in the chapter, "Bugs in the walls, Flies in the Kee Wee Kar Wah.")

My heart bleeds red, white, and blue as I cry when the Supreme Court of conservatives fucks over Americans. Oh God, how can Constitutional principles be determined when health care reform is compared in context with vegetables. Please God, show mercy on me and others who shouted, "Leave the brother alone." We were fooled royally as we thought a black skin on the highest court would benefit our purposes. White America knew the man, black America only saw skin color. The media supported him in framing a beautiful black lady, and he got the job. He wanted to be admired and went back to the little southern town to brag. The media circus will make homecoming pleasing and gratitude will be granted because he put the town on the map. A statue, street, or building will be named after him like the segregationist before.

He did not announce returning in fear a welcoming committee with a rope and a plot in the sewer run-off called drowning nigger hole would be reserved for him. He grew up here, and thanks to a program, he will deny others "affirmative actions." Let him escape. The good white people do not take kindly to black people trying to act as whites, and his life expectancy is less than 1 percent. He is married to a white woman. He parked in front of the courthouse with the two-story Confederate flag. The locals, black and white, would not make eye contact. They prejudged him as an uppity outsider coming to stir up trouble. Clues are the brand-new car and the white shirt. He has been gone to long and forgot or was full of himself. Hometown Negroes were frowned upon for having anything white on—shirts, T-shirts today, white woman tomorrow. Preventive measure a date with the grim reaper and buried in the sewer sink hole. Distorted and second-guessing why he came back to this one-horse town where nobody recognized him. He saw an old black lady approaching, whose job over the decades was to welcome newborns in the world and say good-byes to the departed. She knows everyone past and present in town. He will break the trend and speak first. "How are you doing, Ms. Mattie?"

She answered, "Clarence, Clarence, is that you?"

"Yes, ma'am!"

"You know, the sugar is high, and my eyes playing tricks on me, so come closer, baby. I want to see what a 'real Uncle Tom' look like!"

He left town and swore not to come back. After the funeral, during mingle and meal, she told of the encounter. She told the mourners, "Since we are surrounded by death, I'll tell y'all what I told his mama when he was born. 'He has the black cloud sign of the Judas Goat and will cause more harm to Negroes than good. Take that chicken wire and strangle his black ass now!' Mother instinct always overrule, and she pleaded his case, which was better than any case he ever trampled over. Her words came from the heart. I said, 'Clarence mama, Judas betray Jesus, and you know the story well, so the goat make a ruckus in the slaughterhouse yard. All eyes on him, down a path he goes, and the cattle follows. He duck in a cutaway as the fool cattle continue on, and death for meat lovers. Since born under the sign of an animal, you can make him a follower instead of a leader. You can make him a wolf in sheep clothing. Do not give him breast, cow, or goat milk. The changing solution is give him 'pig milk' as a baby. A toddler go behind the outside toilets get rabbit tobacco and make sassafras tea. The last thing, pray for the devil child out of fear the man becoming.'"

Amazingly, Judas in the picture *The Last Supper* and the goat always are depicted black. America, do spotted or white Judas goat exist? I am sure as the supreme wolf in sheep's clothing. Remember the outcome of Bush versus Gore. The 2010 elections winners were the trailer park tea party Republicans, and the ending name only can be said by white people, "Trash." The trailer park tea party Republicans Trash are motivated to teach America a lesson for reaching out to a black man with an exotic name for help. We dare America challenges are put in the hands of a black and overshadow a white man, who just happens to be dumb-witted. Mr. Dumb's (W) only fault we hold dear is he lowered the student loan interest rates; however, he helped our affiliates gain riches by sending American loved ones to fight and die in vain. Old Shotgun Vice President screwed America as a member of Haliburton cash in on beans and bullets for the wars. When it comes to misleading America with fear of the unknown, Old Shotgun is heartless.

The lie was put forth by ancestors: no matter the circumstances, the color of the skin will determine the outcome. White America needs to be reminded of the circumstances and vote white man rule no matter the grounds he stand for. A black person in politics is detrimental to our way of life. White America needs to keep both feet on the throat of the downtrodden. Let up the pressure and they will look for a deliverer and make him in their likeness, as prescribed in the holy book, Kinky Hair and Black Skin. The day a black person assumes any office will be the start-up date to show what we are made of. (The day the president was sworn into office, a meeting was held to enforce this principle. Refer to the SS (secret society) as mentioned through this passage. The name of the story is, "Bugs in the Walls, Flies in the Kee-Wee-Kar-Wah.") We will resist and tear down America before we defile our parentage. A black is not the answer we want our children to believe. At earnest Mr. Words Without Knowledge old missing top lip of the Senate is feeling the pain and will let his intentions known. He does not care if Americans have jobs, food, or shelter; nothing will be done to support a black in office. The fear the highest office in the land will become the NBA. Including the professionals' first priority, a must have, white women.

The close-minded SS (secret society) believe the hype provided by the black drivers, domestics and others within ear range. A black will never be president, so we are for Hillary. It will be like the good years with Bill. They told us what we wanted to hear and pull a rope, a dope. We need to find a way to see how Colin and Condi voted. Blacks are learning the tool of trade in politics, and our SS (secret society) got it wrong as usual. Our mind-set is stuck in the grand old party days and the inkling to grasp the young minds with technology propel a first black president.

The SS (secret society) have many accomplishments while keeping the office of the president pure white. First on the record was easy. The chief Secret Service guy was in love with the president's wife and wanted him out of the way, so we had the cooperation and eliminated him in Dallas. Another cherished feat is when Martin Luther (rodent) took on the agenda of the poor people— Vietnam war. He laid the groundwork for becoming the first black president. We eliminated him in Memphis by our cohorts, the police department. Run, Jesse, Run! We thought seeking the office would be laid to rest; however, a true candidate came with all the goods—Al Sharpton. We put into play the concepts that got "Run Jesse Run" our media force. The basis he is after the million dollars allotted to serious purposely white candidates for president. My fellow SS (secret society) members, we had to eat shit when we, sic, the IRS on him, and he delivered with a challenge. You do not trust a black man, so count it! The IRS officials wore the badge of chicken-shit not proudly. They were told in advance that he is walking through New York City with no bodyguards, pushing a handcart with a million bucks. Like The Million Man March, droves of people walked with him to witness history. A black man was telling the IRS to sublimely "kiss his ass." Outsiders from New Jersey tried to cause malady, take the money, and run. A spokesman from the Governor's Office recording the event, confronted a bystander, whom he perceived to be a dangerous gangster by his attire (hoodie sweatshirt, armed with a can of Ice Tea and a bag of Skittles candy.) The instigator put a mike in his face and shouted, "Why you don't take the damn money!"

He replied, "Man that's too much money. I only need twenty dollars to rock!"

"Since you stalked, followed, and tried to start a ruckus, this interview costs you twenty dollars. Give it up as I introduce you to the Ice Tea can."

"Sir, meet Mr. Whup Ass with the easy opening."

"Put the mike down! Go bring the white cop standing on the corner. I will give you an extra twenty dollars and my equipment back to you."

"Excuse me, Officer! That black man said, 'I bring you back where he is, he will give me forty dollars.'"

"Mister, my life is on edge over here. You think I am protecting that black man or he's protecting me? Before you answer, I must show some respect. Hey DEE, where my dog's at! Roof! Roof! Now if he asked you to buy a book, the answer will likely be no. He does not like rejection, and to keep from opening the can, he spared you an ass-kicking. You just purchased his autobiography. I just happen to have an extra one, and it's a free pass over here. I guarantee after reading his autobiography, you will drop to your knees and thank God you was not shot. You went into his space, and being white-skinned, you can be kill because he is standing his ground. Here, the book is yours. However you need another piece of information. You have to get it autograph and learn a rhyme. This will cost you twenty dollars. Don't look so dejected. This is a new day in your life. A president got caught up just like you. He did not pay the extra twenty, 'cause, all the Secret Service were order to buy books. Mainstream got it wrong. This is not the 'Big Apple.' Everybody here rhymes. It's called the 'Big Rapper.' When coming here, bring your autograph book with this rhyme. The president have a nickname you must use."

"I'm a white man like Bubba. I'm here not looking for trouble."

"You know the fat Kats, Kittens Klan of Congress wanted him dead because his friend and adviser is black. He came back with his autograph book and move in a living office on Fifth Avenue in Harlem. He's like gold in Fort Knox. You have any problem in the city, do not call the police. We cannot help you. I gave you the tools to live by. After showing the book and rhyme. A true New Yorker will look you in the eye and say, 'The problems we have is no Moe. Our motto here is 'kiss my ass, let it go!' This in mind, give the twenty. I have to go witness a man of God tell the IRS, 'Kiss him where the good Lord split him.'"

The IRS are faced with a "no way out" situation. Reverend Al Sharpton grandstand and James Brown dance all over their faces. The nine, nine, nine, pizza guy has not been approached to give the money back because he is backed by a terrorist group—our right-wing associates, the trailer park tea party Republicans Trash white pussy; I mean white people. The SS (secret society) candidate president Newt is off-limits. He played us like smoking a cheap cigar. Make a showing for president. Sidetrack, get Secret Service tax payer transportation, sell children's books, and payoff of past due services for fucking over Americans in Housing Urban Development Program, Freddie and Fannie Mae. He got money from Mr. frog his sugar daddy in Las Vegas. A conflict of interest we for the party the southern cracker barrel bastard is for himself.

The black president is likeable with celebrity status, yet his wife is more popular. We learned a lesson: family members are off-limits; going after her popularity cost us votes. We threw the obstruction plan, and he rebounded, singing a song, "Let's Stay Together." He backed us in a corner. Oil companies fleeced Americans, raking big profits, and we gave them billions. Tax breaks for the wealthy, and the weeper of the house called student aid, women health money a slush fund. He came back slow jamming (close smooth dance) the issues with a man of comedy, Mr. Jimmy Fallon. I can only speak for myself and not the other SS (secret society) members. "I do not like the taste of shit!" (Some narrating is a man after the weeper of the house job. He strongly believes the weeper is spineless and wants to be a black man because of his tanning habits and his home state motto, "Can't beat them, join them." He urged the president to tax tanning salons as a put-down to the weeper of the house.)

The weeper of the house gave chances of winning slim to none to the world instead of behind closed doors. The trailer park tea party Republicans Trash white pussy, I mean white people's jobs are questionable. The only thing done by this separate arm of the Republican party is sign up for taxpayer-funded health care for their families. This group held America hostage like terrorists and brought forth no legislation. The reply when asked, "We only work forty-one days out of the year. We come to work on Tuesday at twelve noon. We stop work on Thursday at twelve noon and face with an upcoming mandatory five-week vacation. We are not allotted time. Rome was not built overnight. We promise, keep electing us, we will change this (wink, wink)." In contrast, this organization's symbol is not the eagle, it's a skunk!

Robert McLean

The party of No, must preserve the white race by any means. The lower level fights on women, the poor, immigration, sexual orientations, and say, "Its a myth." The highest level keep the 1 percent mega wealthy happy by giving them tax breaks at the expense of education, policeman, fireman, and destruction of the middle class. Preserve this segment of society because this is true white power.

Bugs in the Walls, Flies in Kee-Wee-Kar-Wah (Eternal Bliss)!

The FBI building overshadows the pricey steak house. Electronic listening devices called bugs are placed in every building in Washington DC except the White House. The number one newspaper in the world has it covered, the *National Enquirer*. The unauthorized bugging operations are a need to know and contents cannot be acted on for twenty-five years. By design or careless transcript were not log and file.

The code word for information to be retrieved from the steak house is called "Kee-Wee-Kar-Wah." These are the first words spoken by children of color. The word is deciphered as "Key Your Car." If this ever happens to you, the first response is, "O Shit!" (Today if asked for identification to exercise your right to vote, the word for "O no shit" is "Kee-Wee-AN-Kar Wah.")

The only transparency in Washington DC are domestic workers. Mr. George Willis is a relative of the security guard who exposed Watergate clean and tidied the operation room. It was a learning experience of how his uncle was treated and never compensated. He will not depose any information not related to the secret meeting because of job security and he likes living. The two things his uncle lost—job and the will to live. Uncle Fred was offered a large sum of money; however, he had to travel down this long dark alleyway to a light with a man who looked like Tricky Dick. At the family reunion, we asked why he did not take Mr. Smith-Wesson (gun) and get the money offer with life insurance. He said, "My name is Willis, not Hoffa. Family, listen up. I'm going to instill a family motto to 'live by while working for the government.' During the right thang will get you nut-thang!"

The meeting of the SS (secret society) is called to order. Let me have your attention! I have a message from the originator of this prestige event. The gentleman from the foothills of Kentuck (he dropped the y because of the word "Yankee." He loves the ending k because of his Klan upbringing), Mr. Words Without Knowledge— he stated as leader of the party he has to go to the functioning of The Black Guy. Your attendance make you a true conservative and not one of his flunky fans who ambitions are finding out how he amass over fifty million dollars in only twelve years of public service. (Not to be *alarm*. This is the *norm*. This matter pursue by the Justice Department a standing government would be highly unlikely. Check Issa credentials!) He came from the foothills of Kentuck with meager income, the shirt on his back, and now he is the most powerful man in the world. Mr. Words Without Knowledge goal is to make the *Time Magazine* man of the year, like his mentor in 1936, Adolf Hitler. They express the ideology, the white race are superior in all endeavors. His idol sat in the stadium and watch a slave grandson in front of the world destroy his conception he held to be truth. The greatest Olympian of all times Mr. Jesse Owens won four gold medals. The devil son said, "The black guy will not have four golden years, not on my watch."

Mr. Words Without Knowledge said, "We must stick together, divided we fall. All those with sugar daddies start licking and sucking now, not later." The Black Guy out-raised us. He have millions of donors. We only have your sugar daddies and two countries who host American jobs. They will be able to buy elections, give mega-money, and not be identified. Our motto will be "Corporations are people to my friend." Our investment in shoddy people in powerful positions are paying dividends. We have bought the soul of two Interprets of the Constitution. I am instructed to tell the members of the SS (secret society) how this was accomplish. We are the outreached arm of government and have the means to render services from any individual noteworthy.

The weak judges met in Florida with the Crotch brothers, Itchy and Scratchy. They were separate at the mansion. The judges are like night and day but have one thing in common—vegetables. Itchy Crotch showed he is not impartial and ask Judge Night first, "You want the money or the villa on the island?" Judge Night is cautious and said, "I will not use the 'M' word in your house. I will call it 'lettuce.' I grew up poor, and my wife love lettuce. She is Jewish, you know." He is looking at the money in the trunk. Scratchy Crotch put a date rape pill in his glass of wine. Now the saying "loose lips sink ships." (*Wow*, Mr. Words Without Knowledge top lip became loose from talking too much shit and went away.) Judge Night said, "This wine taste like I got a mouth full of grapes." Itchy Crotch say, "A bottle is ten thousand dollars, and with you under our wings, you can afford it." "I don't know, sir, my lettuce lover would kill me." The date rape pill started to function as prescribe. He became loose with the lips. "Since I am now the official black sheep of the family, I will reveal immediately my family secret. I put lettuce all over the bed, only Benjamin. She wallowed all over them and put my two month wearing boxers on her head. Yes, she has me wear them for two months, and it reminds me of my army life. The Sargent would say, 'Men, it's being a week in the field, now change drawers.' We flip them over! 'Honey, when I do this, what is the metaphor?' 'I do not know.' She said, 'Well, for a judge, you are a little dense. When I roll around the money with your shit-stained drawers on my head, I am saying I love being filthy rich! Now come over here, my big black stallion, and give me a golden shower while telling me how you are going to vote on Civil Rights.' I obliged and said, 'Sweetheart, you know Civil Rights are not for nigger!'" He laughed like no tomorrow.

Itchy and Scratchy Crotch are too rich to have a sense of humor. They need one, they will buy it; everything comes with a price. As judge Night lost control laughing and break dancing on the floor, they quietly excuse themselves. The proposition put forth, Judge Day say he will take the villa. "I made the decisive vote on eminent domain after receiving a large amount of money from China's Wall Mart. Corporations can take your homes, and now a left-wing corporation called The Four M's (Movie Mogul Michael Moore) have bought surrounding property. My house is next, so I am taking the villa. I may need a place for my finally days on earth." Itchy Crotch said, "Oh hell, you are a white man, we will give you both, you deserves better. We are flying you down in your personal jet, a gift from us to see a bit of paradise. If you are thinking about "Dark man" do not be concern. Our background checks of you two candidates reveal an important fact. We deem you more important by reading the many reviews you have written. The Dark man literally have us in the dark. Many years on the bench no record standing of ever writing one. Chief Justice should had order him to do a review on Civil Rights. The bench first all agreement in history and the only Negro opposed. He told us the story and admitted his wife saying, 'For a judge, you are a little dense.'" (Reader, did you come to the conclusion that name-calling was racially motivated at first?)

When he got to the island, his first request—get rid of the beautiful split tails. Go in the jungle deep and bring back three-leg savages. The villa will be called, My Savages. The transistor operator whose job is reporting to the brothers things that happens or don't. Sirs, an incident happen which needs to be squashed before Interpol or the *National Enquirer* get involve. The judge feels he has been robbed. He say the beautiful man look like the movie star in *Saturday Night Fever* and would like a massage for thirty-five dollars. After service was rendered, he wanted to pay him in local currency, which translated to thirty-five cents. (Today the Candy Company, two bags for a dollar, from the racist state of South Carolina resides here. Natives work eighteen hours a day for fifty dollars, local. Translation: fifty cents American. American lives destroyed by greed. Take a family trip to the town east of Manning South Carolina and look at the giant gray ex-Candy complex, which was once a beacon for America.) John took forty dollars out of his money belt and called the police. Thirty-five dollars for the service as promised and five dollars for the police trip. The police did not charge John because a robber would had taken all his money. This bastard had 9999.99 dollars The police ask why he had that much money. He replied, "I voted on the law I do not have to declare any amount under ten thousand. Knowing the law enable rich people like me to fuck over the United States Government with the many loopholes provided." The police left with a warning. "Look, do not touch the beautiful native men until he learn customs and courteous." He adhere to the warning. All he does is watch the men dipping his vegetable in ranch dressing. He does not bite the vegetable, just suck and swallow. "Eric, my doctor told me to help with my weight." "After twelve noon, eat carrots with dressing." I bet the doctor told him the same thing. "Newt, you would lose the bet. The vegetable dipped not bitten, suck and swallow is brocoli." "Eric, the bet, double or nothing." Since he got rid of the ladies, I bet the part of the vegetable he relate to is the stem, not the flower. "Newt, never double dare, unless you check your fact meter. (Words of wisdom given by a newly elect President Clinton to a four-year racist radio journalist. Today he still do not check the fact meter and say outlandish things like 'The Democrats kill (Mr.) Emit Till.') Wrong again, Newt, both, he is bi-sexual."

"Eric, you say we have the 2012 election in the bag all sewn up. I'm running for president. The first thing on the plate is make the judges accountable for their rulings. They do not interpret the Constitution. They only look up 'In God We Trust' on Benjamin Franklin ass on the hundred-dollar bill. My faith is limited with these cohorts. Anybody can buy them. We did. In case something happen and I'm not nominated in 2012, I want our shoo in president to put me on his cabinet. I want to be Secretary of the zoo." Paul said, "What is up with you and animals?" "Well, Paul, I like to be around elephants and the giant killer whales. They make me feel small, and I like the feeling. The main reason is the sensitively they endure. They are more nice than the Northers in the Republican party the APA—you know, the Arrogant Pompous Assholes." The baffled look on Paul's face made Newt laugh like there was no tomorrow.

Mr. Words Without Knowledge said, "Stick together. We are above the law. Get on committees to create jobs and obstruct. Preach unstable rhetoric such as war on women, welfare, students, immigration, voter suppression, and keep the Justice Department on the defense. Put into play his theories, guesswork, speculations, and pivotal bullshit. We will set the tone for blacks and women. The office of the president of the United States is not for you."

He will show his majesty power and prove to the SS (secret society) he is above the law of the land. He will announce six days after the Black Guy is in office, "Americans, you people are stupid. I do not care about swearing an oath to upholding the Constitution. Hell, I do not care about jobs, life, love for country, welfare of citizens, or the pursuit of happiness. My only concern—a black man will only serve one term as president. We the people are going to make his life a living hell. This is what true Americans want."

Eric asked, "Anymore business we need to discuss?" Paul spoke up. "I got a call from the colored man, the RNC chairman. The party paid for this meal and brought to his attention the meal is pricey. I explain we are buying privacy, not the six-hundred-dollar six-ounce steaks. We are in the shadows of the FBI across the street. We are saving the party money. Newt took care of the meal and sent you the bill. He said, 'That all good, so do the fuzzy math and explain to me, a real dumb-ass, how fourteen people can eat one hundred fourteen watermelons at a thousand dollars apiece.' Newt, we trusted you. We forgot your love of animals and you acting like a dog chasing his tail, a damn Southern politician." Newt smiled and said, "Paul, you can call me anything, but, late for supper, motherfucker. This is a springboard for 2012. I will settle then, now I have a bus to catch. I am going to Las Vegas to do some licking and sucking. I just want to say, 'Bye-bye Miss America pie. I am bus to the levy, but, the levy was dry. We good old boys drinking whiskey and rye. This is the day the Black Guy die.' As a known lover of animals, I bid farewell as I depart. See y'all later, alligator. After while crocodiles, and for you Paul. After supper, motherfucker. Stay seated men. You only have to rise in 2012, when I'm president of the United States and the band play my song, 'Hail to the Thief.'"

On behalf of the fearless leader, Eric thanked the only outsider, Mr. Goldstein, an executive producer of Fox News for the steady support on conservatives issues and renown bullshit. He said, "I have full blessing of my network to handle public relations. I see the first on the horizon when Mr. Words Without Knowledge tell America go fuck yourselves. We need to call on former governors who have nothing to gain or lose. Tell America people in politics, we say this all the time. We should be aware what we are doing is sick, twisted, and smell like treason." Thank God we are not in China. Don King, a boxing promoter, would say, "Only in America we have the audacity to do this and live to talk about it." (W) killed America, and we support the Black Guy an iota. He will be the epitome of the office and a picture etch on Mount Rushmore. After (W) you can only go up. We must compare his actions with Mr. Thousand Dollar Boots never (W). The mind-set will be like The Black Guy playing cards with us. Stipulation he wears a blindfold, handcuff in the back, and we have all the aces. We should also tie him up. He might possess the Houdini feats like the black man handcuff in the back. He is in the back of an Arkansas police car. He shot himself in the head. The right temple to be exact. However, he is left-handed. He was searched twice. Chief said, "He hid the weapon in his ass and commit suicide." As a man of the media, I contradict the reporting of the episode by the Arkansas Press. They say he was sandwiched between two white men. Change the gender and his death is justifiable on the whim of an evil cop, who is determined to take the country back on request of the conservative radio hosts.

We must corral the bigot racist radio journalists to tone down the negative rhetoric. Tea party animals and right-wing nut jobs will follow suit. Shoot women and children, the key to existence on their request to take the country back. The sad thing, lawmakers have taxpayers' insurance, and the American women and children will not. I say a sleeping dog might bite you if you wake him up. Let America continue to sleep. We deter jobs away, the economy sucks, the blame game is in full effect: it's the Black Guy fault. As a Jew who goes through life saying, "I got my mind on my money and my money on my mind," we need to tell the conservative radio hosts they sound really stupid saying the economy is fucked up. In the same breath stating for facts, corporations are sitting on trillions of dollars, waiting to see how the Black Guy will tax their money. Men, this is un-American bullshit! They need to shit can talking about the trillions of dollars setting offshore waiting for tax exemptions. The money is now dormant. In American banks it will draw interest, compound daily paid by the government. The tax and interests offset. Only draw interest without taxation is downright unpatriotic greed. We should not get full of ourselves. Americans are not stupid!

Our radio comrades, Rush, Mike, Sean, Laura, Glen and the wannabes should stick with the one expertise exemplified, name-calling. They are hiding behind the mike. One brave soul who suppose to be here is hiding in the fort he call home. He leaked word he is too popular and the SS (secret society) would be expose. My gut feelings say he is just a blow hard and just maybe a left-wing nut job will make him pay for his bigot racist antics. Our television will handle the tough issues. Our master plan: have beautiful ladies with short dresses and no panty lines. After each key issue, they will slowly, methodically cross their legs. Men and some women will lose thought, and the dogs will continue to sleep.

My grandpa lived a lie during the War. He watched and participated in the gassing of his own people (Jews). The Gestapo would come and look in his blue eyes and give the same ideology express today. "Our plan is marvelous, but we cannot tell anyone." I will leave with this "Power to the party!" Out of hearing range, Eric said, "Thank God that Jesus killer is on our side."

Heavy lines appeared on Paul's forehead, a sign of dejection. Eric asked, "What's going on, good buddy" (homosexual term used by truck drivers, faggot)?

"Our fearless leader, Mr. Words Without Knowledge is obsessed with the Black Guy and reference sticking together apply with him only, right? I have a personal issue with that Southern cracker barrel bastard. He know just enough to be dangerous as president. He stated, 'The judges who ruling affect all Americans will be held accountable and must report to him.' We worked hard putting reliable contractors in place to rule in our favor always. He used black profanity and thought attractive to call me, a white man, a motherfucker. Eric, he bitch-slapped us by inflating the meal and dare us to do anything. The food probably came from his trashy trailer park in Georgia. He is still fighting the War Between the States and will not surrender. He treats everyone who resides north of the Mason Dixon Line like shit.

"Our donors are racists, and his sugar daddy, Mr. Frog, is the hop of the litter (ha-ha). While he is busing, I'm flying to drop some dimes (give pertain information). His conduct as a Southern gentleman is questionable. Just maybe, while licking, sucking he bite, and his sugar daddy will not buy the office for him in 2012. I will suggest giving him enough money to show face. Limited funds, he will drop from the race. The test of time will be if he say, 'I'm going for the "Gusto." I'm using my wife money to stay in contention.' Not likely this will ever happen. A true politician cannot grasp using own resources (prime example: taxpayer-funded health care). Eric, if he get wind of me interfering in his dream and confronts me, I will show him we have great politicians north of the Mason Dixon Line also. I will look him in the eye and tell him a lie."

Eric walked away and mumbled, "You arrogant, pompous, asshole, motherfucker."

Note: This is a satire. People, places, names, likeness, are coincidental and *only* exist for real in "The twi-light zone." God Bless the Black Guy and the SS (secret society).

Robert McLean

OPENLY DISGRACE IN YOUR FACE (CLOSING)

Openly disgrace acts of Congress are plentiful. It's amazing, how they find the time with the feeble work week. It dawned on me as a former soldier. I had, like many others who found a home in the military, two sets of gear, field and inspection. Congress is depicted likewise: clean or dirty. The end of this chapter will pay homage to the collective "dirt." The above question will be answered entirely.

Some in-your-face moments that wretch foul odors. Big Oil raking in large profits, give them billions. Jobs, no legislation to stop or slow, outsource to other countries. A man with dual citizenship will give up being an American, so he will not have to pay a fair share of tax. An act of treason can happen anywhere, even in the Hall of Congress. This comment received a standing ovation. "Shame on me! Shit on you!" What a great bluff. Singapore, his money becomes the government. He needs to insult (Right word, voice change when ask about tax returns. IRS wanted to crucify me for 888 dollars. I did my taxes and used the wrong line. How can a rich man go ten years without paying taxes? Appears some people are above the law.) a man running for the highest office in the land for advice on protecting overseas financial matters. One more as spoken by this racist bigot radio journalist, "No use beating a dead trigger." Congress voted universal health care for Iraq. Are they really saying these people deserve better than Americans (ask your official)? Children in movie theater shot by an evil person touch a nerve; this is our future generation. They do not have what our lawmakers have, insurance. Would a safety net be put in place if these were lawmakers' children or grandchildren? The hospitals will absorb short-term care; however, military people understand long-range care is warranted. Lawmakers used the phrase what the American people, want repeal and replace. I can only speak for myself, "Repeal health care and replace with yours!" (It's proven.)

America should vote each presidential year health care for Congress, yes or no by popular demand. We can have a write in for lawmakers

238

to be exempt. My choice would be a lady denied coverage because of a preexisting condition. "This bitch is crazy!"

The phone rang at 3:00 a.m., and the caller said, "We are even, sir."

"God bless you, John, for doing the right thing."

"Sorry for bothering you this time of the morning, sir. I thought you would rather hear it from the horse's mouth instead of the horse conservative ass."

He chuckled, "John you got supreme jokes and full of surprises. This is my quiet time. I read and monitor the phone. You got a minute. I would like to share something with you."

"I don't know, sir. I dial you by mistake. I'm trying to get the 900 number and did not have my glasses on."

"Again, John, you got supreme jokes and should show your 'Ron Paul' (explanation later) side more often." My better half honors quiet time. To keep from disturbing me, she gets gear from Mr. Fred, X cap (Spike Lee sent over 10,000 for the Easter Egg Roll) triple X Howard University sweatshirts, shades, and browses around Home Depot. I shout from the highest office, "I love my wife!" A share secret John. "You can take her out of Chicago, but you cannot take Chicago out of her. She tried me and put on the Chicago 'Fling Thing' of all places, Oregon. She hit me with her plan to go out during quiet time. I said, 'We will discuss it when we get back to DC.' She demanded an answer, 'Now!' I think the popularity thing kicked in. You know, she is more popular. Told her politely, 'Get in the car. We will discuss it later.' 'No, I want your answer now!' I just had a bad bowling tenure and now this. 'Let's go, driver!' We were airborne over Idaho and things were tense on Air Force One. We are a close-knit group, and I thought they were feeling my pain. I noticed they were looking at the time clocks. I said, 'Man, turn this thing around! I left something very important.' People started cheering and throwing hundred-dollar bills on Hillary. She bet all takers, the plane would be ordered to turn around in ten minutes or less. Hillary said, 'Mr. President, I am hoping you come to your senses a lot quicker.' I only had one minute to spare. I reached for my wallet, She waved me off and said, 'I got your back.' John, this remarkable lady slip the money to her aide and said, 'For the beautiful baby.' I went back. My precious jewel was still pouting and standing on the corner. Date night in New York City I said, 'Oh hell, yell to my one in a million.' John, the neighbors know her name! I did not hear a whimper, right?"

"Shucks, sir. You know judges don't cry. Continue on!"

"I read an editorial in *Time* magazine written by a Hispanic gentleman who said, 'Republicans are bugged-eyed and shouting the president is playing politics with immigration, women's rights, students, and health care.' I love the analog he used, compared me with Mr. LeBron James. Here goes, if you put Mr. LeBron James on a basketball court with a basketball, what are the expectations? I am playing politics, duh, I'm a damn ordinary politician! The only thing that separates me from the Rethuglicans is, 'I think Jesus is cool.' (Thanks, Mr. Anthony Hamilton.) They need to stay bugged-eyed, stop shouting, and hear what I am saying. Your eyes and ears should work together. Only once in my life they did not contrast. I am watching the late Mr. Rodney King encountered with the police. I'm hearing the narration, 'He's taking his head beating the police batons.' John, it's early morning, go ahead, man, laugh out loud. I finished reading a twofer, and the outcomes are great. Its two books combined, and the author admits taking the idea from 'The Great One,' Mr. Walter Moseley. I'm sending you nine copies. The books highlight hate, hope, and love. I got more than my share of hate and hope from Congress. The author gave me and you the solution in regard to obtaining love from Congress. It comes from the greatest band in the land Maze, featuring Mr. Frankie Beverly. He said, 'I got myself to remind me of love.' John, love yourself, man. America needs you above the ignorance of the bench."

"How true, sir. I will say goodnight with your slogan. 'Got your back one time.'"

"John, in life and politics, one time, one chance, one shot, is all you need. My super team strives only get health care on first base. Once America comes to the plate and sees through the smoke screen provided, a home run will prevail. Women and children shot, no fault of their own, will be able to buy cars, homes, and have credit. Medical billings will not hindrance, and they can live productive lives. We the people will take care of our own!"

Washington's ways of during things may not be illegal, but damn right disgraceful. This element of the fat Kats, Kitten Klan of Congress is the most dangerous. This collective dirt are called by their peers, "the dirty hands group." The DHG are enslaving (hate word) Americans by wheeling and dealing behind close triple-locked doors. Their motto is, "Out of sight, out of mind." They are the givers of society, always passing the stuffed envelopes at midnight as described by a man of comedy, Mr. Jay Leno. The only time exposed by the most-feared newspaper in the world, the *National Enquirer*. A member in the men's public toilet is thought to adhere to the posted sign. Looking for sex tap six times. He denied the incident, and he is gay. He resigned without clearing his name. Revealing actions of the DHG results in penalty for you and family members' death. The tap code was for a judge in the next stall waiting for his "lettuce" (money). The detective literally jumped the gun. If he had waited a few seconds more, he would had witnessed a response of six taps. After taking down the judge also, all-black America would line up, shake his hand, and say, "Thank you." The culprit slipped away like a thief in the dark man (previous encountered). The DHG are not gangsters. They just have gangsters ways: greed, money, power, and the big kicker. Fucking over Americans with direct emphasis on the highest office in the land.

The beautiful CNN commentator with the exotic name guest is a person wearing the title of "Actor." His brothers are well known;

however, his works are suspect. He is getting exposure to the media because of his name-calling the president a gangster. She asked, "Why you call him that?" He said this three time throughout the interview. "I call it as I see it." (Making this statement, attention is brought to his eyes which play a greater part of his ideology. They are slanted and close to his nose. Appearance and stupidity, I will prejudge him as being, "nearsighted.") She is too smart to let him off the hook with this lame reasoning. "You are a supporter of the non-taxpaying man running for the highest office in the land." He says he will only show his returns after elected. Maybe as president he can pardon the IRS official that took his bribes. I will call it as I see it. I say, "This is a real-life gangster. We will compare the two." "Why you call the president a gangster?" "Well, he is from Chicago, and he went behind closed doors to get 'Health Care' started." She gave him the look, yes the look: "I am beautiful, but slap me silly."

"This is it? You label him, and if I am a chair, this would not have legs to stand on."

I remember a saying from my childhood, "Wat a idiot." The shakers and movers in American politics do best work behind closed doors. Color of skin dictates superiority, so the devils will not come to you take your message to hell and back. I will give the so-called actor a leg to stand on. I highly suggest taking a course, Name-Calling 101 from the media genic experts. Little boy (rush), tar baby (Michelle), beans and rice (Sean), black meat, meat (Sarah), kill babies (Laura), Jew Killer (Glenn), Ammo loaded (Paul V.), Holocaust happen I'm a Jew (Neil) and a slew of wannabe that slither from under the same racist, bigot rock.

Taking the plan to the "Lime lighters" or the ones present only when a camera is available is wishful thinking. He took the right course of actions and has nothing to be ashamed of. The so-called actor should continue walking in his brother's footsteps, this is the only way he will continue "living the good life."

Note: Closing this book with information from a church sign in the great country of Texas. You see they have "The Un-constitutional Doctrine." They emplace bylaws, laws, and governing people not conducive to American beliefs and values. The great country of Texas has been hit with many "natural acts" because "God do not like ugly." The country has its own language called, "Spoken Texas." A challenge motto is, "Do not mess with Texas, we will fuck you up." The country symbol is not the "Longhorn" cattle. It's an easy-to-open can called, "Mr. Whup Ass."

Leaving Houston routed for Shreveport on Highway 59. Up the hill, around a curve, a small town approaches. Immediately noticeable on the left is a strategic place sign, leaning on a white row house (called shotgun in my youth, shoot from the front through the back, a straight house). The lumber and paint should have been used for repairing the rundown houses. The sign is as large as the house and leaning on it, it carried the name, "Ron Paul." I came to the conclusion the side the sign is leaning is the funny side of the house. On my right is a red brick church. All churches are beautiful. The sign summed it for all. It read, "God Bless *Our* America."